THE
PUZZLEMASTER
P R E S E N T S

200 Mind-Bending Challenges

FROM NPR®

by Will Shortz

with an introduction by Liane Hansen

**Random House
Puzzles & Games**

Most of the puzzles that appear in this work were originally broadcast on
National Public Radio®'s *Weekend Edition*® *Sunday* from 1987 through 1996.

This work was originally published in 1996 by Times Books,
a division of Random House, Inc.

ISBN 0-8129-6386-5

Random House Puzzles & Games website address:
www.puzzlesatrandom.com

Text design and typography by Mark Frnka
Manufactured in the United States of America

9

INTRODUCTION

Listeners to NPR's *Weekend Edition Sunday* are not what you would call shy. Every week we receive letters, phone calls, and e-mail that excoriate us for the opinions of our analysts, examine in minute detail our grammar and usage, express gratitude for our reports on meaningful issues, or extol the virtues of their own political or personal philosophies. But the schoolteacher in Illinois; the chemist in California; the actor in New York City; and the lawyer in North Carolina all have one thing in common. Call it the highest common denominator. Their correspondence invariably ends with "P.S. Love the puzzle." In fact, one midwestern gentleman said his horses chew more contentedly when our Puzzlemaster is on the air.

Will Shortz is a founding father of the *Weekend Edition Sunday* family. Ten years ago Susan Stamberg, radio goddess, national treasure, and original host of this program, wanted a puzzle to be a part of the show. As the crossword puzzle is a given in Sunday newspapers, so an audio puzzle would be an integral part of our program. At first it was a game between Susan and Will. When I joined the family in 1989, we invited listeners to play.

My seven minutes with Will are the most challenging and invigorating ones of the week. In the following pages you will discover why. So, clear your mind, expect the unexpected, lighten up, and have fun.

Liane Hansen
Host, *Weekend Edition Sunday*

ACKNOWLEDGMENTS

The author would like to thank:

- Susan Stamberg for conceiving the idea of the *Weekend Edition Sunday* puzzle

- Liane Hansen for providing an abundance of warmth and personality on the air

- Bob Malesky, Fred Wasser, Ned Wharton, and the rest of the *WESun* staff over the years for their help and support

- *Word Ways* magazine (Spring Valley Road, Morristown, NJ 07960) and *The Enigma*, organ of the National Puzzlers' League (P.O. Box 82289, Portland, OR 97282) for frequent inspiration

- Everyone who has tested and polished the *WESun* puzzles over the years, but especially Peter Gordon, David Rosen, Merl Reagle, and Evie Eysenburg

1. BODY LANGUAGE

Each answer in this puzzle is a word that sounds like a letter of the alphabet plus the name of part of the body. What are the words?

Ex. Spirit in a bottle ___genie___ [G + knee]

1. President's "no" ___veto___

2. Chicago airport ___O'hare___

3. Kind of coffee that won't keep you awake ___decaf___

4. Some skid row drunks ___(winos)___

5. What a pizza place can usually do on request ___deliver___

6. Designer Cassini ___Oleg___

7. 1960s-style college protest, as one that a professor might lead (hyph.) ___teach-in___

8. Card game played with a 48-card deck ___p-knuckle___

9. Make sticky and messy ___(begum)___

10. Kind of tax, as on liquor or tobacco ___(excise)___ [Note: The name of the body part in this one is plural.]

Rating Good: 5   Excellent: 7   Ace: 9

---

2. GOING AROUND IN CIRCLES

Starting with the four small o's shown below left, you can turn them into the word "goad" by adding a few lines as shown at right.

o o o o → g o a d

Starting with six small o's, what two common six-letter words can you spell by adding a few lines?

o o o o o o

o o o o o o

3. PLAY IT BY EAR

The name of what sport or game rhymes with each of the following words?

    Ex. Menace   _Tennis_____

    1. Thicket _____

    2. Broker _____

    3. Jockey _____

    4. Trolling _____

    5. Bless _____

    6. Blocker _____

    7. Smidge _____

    8. Pseudo _____

    9. Lingo _____

  10. Solo _____

  11. Wash _____

  12. Harems _____

  13. Blotchy _____

  14. Bouquet _____

  15. Cooker _____

  16. Rouge _____

  17. Nestling _____

  18. [2 answers] Starts _____ _____

Rating   Good: 12 (out of 19)   Excellent: 15   Ace: 18

4. NUT CASE

Take the word FANG. Shift each letter four spaces down the alphabet and you get the word JERK. (That is, F shifted four spaces down the alphabet becomes J, A shifted four spaces down the alphabet becomes E, etc.) Now name a variety of nut in which each letter can be shifted four spaces down the alphabet to name an animal.

5. YOU CAN SAY THAT AGAIN

Fill in each blank below with two homophones (words that are pronounced the same but have different spellings) to complete the sentence.

    Ex. While bullets whizzed overhead in battle, the yellow-bellied _coward cowered_.

1. Helga consumed seven pancakes at the pancake breakfast, but I was so hungry I _____.

2. To get the best bargains in nautical supplies, wait for the next _____.

3. With a full waiting room, and running two hours behind schedule, the doctor was clearly wearing out his _____.

4. Neighing all day long will not make a _____.

5. In the library reference room, is talking _____?

6. To prevent leaks from the overhead apartment, the landlord applied some _____.

7. The oil fields that still have the greatest reserves are the ones that have been _____.

In each of the last three sentences, fill in the blank with three homophones.

8. The older wildebeests were not aware of the zookeeper's evil plans, but the _____.

9. Mortimer's clock said 1:57, and our clock showed three minutes _____.

10. No matter how much we trained the workman in penmanship, we couldn't make the _____.

Rating   Good: 5   Excellent: 7   Ace: 9

---

6. TO THE REAR

What verb has its past tense formed not by adding "-d" or "-ed," but by moving its first letter to the end?

7. "SIR!"

Answer every clue with a word or name beginning with the syllable "sir" (in any spelling).

Ex. Sure thing _certainty_

1. Three-ring event _____
2. Juicy steak _____
3. *The Twilight Zone* host _____
4. Smith, Jones, or Chang, e.g. _____
5. Geometrical figure _____
6. 1973 Al Pacino movie _____
7. Poll _____
8. Enchantress in *The Odyssey* _____
9. Legal writ _____
10. From Belgrade _____
11. First word at a birthday party, maybe _____
12. Kind of station or break _____
13. Hat-shaped diacritical mark _____
14. Operation _____
15. Garden of Eden creature _____
16. Pancake topping _____
17. Kind of mother _____
18. Three-headed dog of myth _____
19. Pianist Rudolf _____
20. Sunday morning message _____

Rating Good: 10   Excellent: 14   Ace: 18

8. "I" ON AMERICA

The 11-letter name of one of the states in the United States consists of the letter I between two words that are opposites of each other. What is it?

9. SHIFTING INTO REVERSE

Answer each clue with a two-word phrase in which the two words are reversals of each other.

Ex. Dull-colored poet   _drab bard_

1. Enthusiastic opera singer   _____

2. Satan existed   _____

3. Smooth and shiny timbers on the bottoms of boats

   _____

4. Send a watch in payment   _____

5. Quick movies sponsored by a popular beer   _____

6. Manufactured Dutch cheese   _____

7. Dust Bowl resident's Japanese watch   _____

8. Drive off an outcast   _____

9. Set down a watch face   _____

10. Comic strip "menace" broke a Commandment   _____

11. Student's mistake   _____

12. Garments made by needlework smell bad   _____

13. Turned toward a kind of coffee   _____

14. Lowers an arachnid again   _____

15. Emphasized cakes, pies, etc.   _____

Rating   Good: 8   Excellent: 11   Ace: 14

---

10. ANIMALS BACKING UP

Think of two animals that have names of three letters each. Put these names side by side and read them backward, and you'll get a common six-letter word. What is it? Here's a hint: The two animal names are general names—not the ones for a particular gender or variety.

11. TWO-IN-ONE

Add a doubled letter somewhere to each of the following six-letter words to get a common eight-letter word.

	Starting Word	Doubled Letter	New Word
Ex.	RULING	F	RUFFLING
1.	COERCE	___	_____
2.	EXCEED	___	_____
3.	POSTER	___	_____
4.	PRIEST	___	_____
5.	STRING	___	_____
6.	AURATE	___	_____
7.	TATTER	___	_____
8.	NEEDLE	___	_____
9.	BUYING	___	_____
10.	DISMAY	___	_____

Rating   Good: 6   Excellent: 8   Ace: 10

---

12. COINING NAMES

Can you find eight or more boys' names or nicknames hidden on a U.S. dime? For example, hidden in the phrase ONE DIME on the back of the coin are the consecutive letters of NED. See if you can find at least seven other familiar boys' names or nicknames. You may use both sides of the coin.

13. S & S

Every answer here is a familiar phrase consisting of two words starting with S separated by the word "and."

Ex. The gist or heart of the matter <u>sum and substance</u>

1. In an old saying, they may break your bones _____
2. The American flag _____
3. 1970s Redd Foxx sitcom _____
4. Unreasonable acts prevented by the Fourth Amendment of the Constitution _____
5. Tortoise's motto for winning the race _____
6. Basic, quick lunch _____
7. Large book publisher _____
8. Variety of magazine perfume ad _____
9. Complete this phrase: "star of ____"(describing an important actor) _____
10. Tennessee Williams play made into a 1961 movie _____
11. Mixed drink sung about by the Kingston Trio _____
12. Competitor of Coppertone _____
13. Extremely clean _____
14. Kind of sauce in a Chinese restaurant _____

Rating   Good: 7   Excellent: 10   Ace: 13

14. S & S, TOO

Think of a seven-letter word that contains two S's in a row. Drop the S's to get a five-letter word that means the same as the longer one. What is it? Hint: The same letter of the alphabet immediately precedes and follows the S's in the longer word.

15. ANIMALISTIC

Here we pay a visit to the Bad Pun Department—reaching way in the back of the department for these. Fill the name of an animal in each blank to complete the sentence in a punny way.

Ex. Someone of your intelligence _____ **otter** _____ know better.

1. If you have to lift your car off the ground to change a tire, this _____ do the trick.

2. In case it's cool on my vacation, _____ warm sweater in my suitcase.

3. She's smart. She's beautiful. She's sweet. She's the _____ my dreams.

4. When my wife asked, "What's the weather like, honey?" I said, "It looks like _____."

5. Is it for beef or mutton you have a hankering, or is it for _____?

6. The crazy millionaire zookeeper, when on his deathbed, _____ his entire estate.

7. Said the father to his departing boy, "_____!"

8. Siskel and Ebert _____ terrible movie and gave it two thumbs down.

9. Quit looking at my test paper, you _____!

10. How much does an antique like that _____?

11. If Joe won $10 million in the lottery, he _____ his boring job in a second.

12. We would love to see our _____ and get hitched to that young man she's been seeing.

Rating   Good: 4   Excellent: 7   Ace: 10

---

16. ANIMAL HEAD

What animal's name, beginning with the letter F, becomes the name of another animal if you drop the first letter?

17. PUZZLE WITH AP-PEAL

Every answer is a word, name, or phrase that contains the syllable BELL somewhere within it.

Ex. Weightlifter's item _____dumbbell_____

1. Ferdinand's queen _____

2. Hotel baggage carrier _____

3. Red-haired clown on *Howdy Doody* _____

4. The navel _____

5. Author of *Herzog* _____

6. French forest, site of a WW1 battle _____

7. Literature regarded as fine art _____

8. Colorful wildflower _____

9. Old-fashioned room heater _____

10. Warlike, or aggressively hostile _____

11. German measles _____

12. Sylvia Plath novel _____

13. Renowned London antique market _____

14. Deadly nightshade _____

15. Male sheep that leads the flock _____

16. Noted American trial lawyer _____

17. Popular '70s pants _____

18. Actor who won a Tony for *Sunrise at Campobello* _____

Rating   Good: 8   Excellent: 12   Ace: 16

---

18. IT'S ELEMENTARY

Think of a two-syllable word that means "elementary." Reverse the syllables phonetically and get a common two-word phrase meaning "a hospital on board a ship." What are the words?

19. MUMBO-JUMBO

A patient at a dentist's office received an Oral Care Home Kit to take with him when he left. Among the items inside was an envelope labeled "plaque removal aid," which, when opened, turned out to contain—this is absolutely true—a toothpick! Thus, a commonly available item that cost less than a penny to make was, through clever labeling, transformed into a distinctive and valuable dental device. Similarly, for each of the following flowery phrases, name the inexpensive, everyday item actually described. Answer lengths are provided in parentheses.

Ex. Plaque removal aid (9)

toothpick

1. Multifurcated coiffeur arranger (4)

2. Perforated epistolary expediter (5)

3. Tubular beverage conduit (5)

4. Cupreous presidential engraving (5)

5. Circular sartorial fastening device (6)

6. Bilateral elongated abrading apparatus (4,4)

7. Rose-colored graphite eliminator (6)

8. Pack of handheld lined oratorical aids (5,5)

9. Combination embroidery tool/direction locater (6)

10. Instant metallic security device disabler (3)

Rating   Good: 4   Excellent: 6   Ace: 8

20. YOU DON'T SAY!

What common five-letter word contains a silent "ch"?

21. TWO G'S

Every answer is a two-syllable word or name in which each syllable starts with the letter G.

Ex. Use Listerine, for example ___gargle___

1. Flock of geese _____
2. Kind of dancer _____
3. French artist in Tahiti _____
4. Welder's eyewear _____
5. 10 to the 100th power _____
6. Snaky-haired monster of myth _____
7. Sound of a water fountain _____
8. Bauble _____
9. Kind of counter _____
10. One of the Khans _____
11. Actor famous for playing Hamlet _____
12. Kind of eyes for the amorous _____
13. More than enthusiastic _____
14. Russian writer, The Father of Russian Realism _____
15. Awkwardly tall _____
16. Girlish laugh _____
17. Decoration on an old building _____
18. Not fully awake _____

Rating   Good: 12   Excellent: 15   Ace: 17

---

22. HEAVY THOUGHTS

The names of what three standard units of weight can follow the prefix "pro-" to complete common words?

PRO_____   PRO_____   PRO_____

23. NAME SCRAMBLE

Rearrange the letters in each of the following words to get a common girl's name.

Ex. SOIL ___LOIS___

1. SALE _____
2. DINE _____
3. WAND _____
4. GOAL _____
5. CAGER _____
6. DAILY _____
7. BYTES _____
8. HOARD _____
9. EVENLY _____
10. AIMLESS _____
11. LEARNED _____
12. RETOTAL _____
13. SEEDIER _____
14. HABITAT _____
15. COLINEAR _____
16. ARMENIAN _____
17. SAILABLE _____
18. ORDINALS _____
19. HERITANCE _____
20. REALIGNED _____

Rating   Good: 8   Excellent: 13   Ace: 18

24. PEN AND INK

Think of a word that contains the consecutive letters P-E-N in order. Change them to I-N-K (also in order) to get a different word. Neither answer word has anything to do with pen or ink. What two words are they?

25. CATEGORIES

Think of an answer for each category at the top of the box beginning with each of the letters A-P-R-I-L. For example, if the category were "Elements," you might say *Arsenic, Phosphorus, Radium, Iron,* and *Lead.* Fill in one answer per space. Your answers do not have to match ours.

	U.S. STATES	THINGS IN A KITCHEN	PARTS OF A CAR	UNITS OF MEASURE	BOOKS OF THE BIBLE
A					
P					
R					
I					
L					

Rating   Good: 14   Excellent: 19   Ace: 24

---

26. IN A JAM

If we asked you: In three letters, what word means both "preserve" and "predicament"?—you might say JAM. What answer might you give in six letters?

27. OXYMORONS

Answer each clue with a two-word phrase in which the two words are opposites of each other.

Ex. Weighty lantern *heavy light*

1. Lowermost spinning toy _____
2. Moonshine machine that makes a racket _____
3. Makes betting probabilities equal _____
4. Leisurely refusal to eat food _____
5. Fairly hideous _____
6. Particular four-star officer _____
7. Not many realty units _____
8. Four-sided leg joint _____
9. Hunky-dory psychiatrist _____
10. License to run a tavern _____
11. Very natty-looking apartment _____
12. Concealed expanse of flat land _____

Rating Good: 4   Excellent: 7   Ace: 10

---

28. CARNIVAL SIGN

An advertisement for a traveling carnival is painted on the wall of an old barn. But some of the paint has peeled off, making a few of the words difficult to read. Here's one of the words that onlookers are having trouble with:

C P C I F S C J L

What word is it? Here is a hint: The F in the middle can represent itself, or it can be an E without the bottom stroke. The answer is an adjective that might describe one of the carnival acts.

29. FOR THE BIRDS

In each sentence, fill in the blanks with two words that will go together to name a bird.

Ex. The thieves intend to __rob__ the museum, provided they can figure out how to get ___in___. [rob + in = robin]

1. We watched the boxers _____ from our first-_____ seats.

2. _____ of the farm is on the other side of the Blue _____ Mountains.

3. Barbie, looking very _____ in her new clothes, had a date with her boyfriend _____.

4. After the guest accidentally dropped the hostess' sterling silver _____ down the drain, the hostess ungraciously sent him a _____ to replace it.

5. When Arnold Palmer says he can't birdie a _____ four hole, that's just _____!

6. It took the domestic _____ almost an _____ to develop its modern "oink."

7. Dad was such a _____, he'd balance a Ritz _____ on the end of his nose.

The final two sentences have three words that combine to form a bird's name.

8. You may have to _____ the _____ old horse if he _____ not pull the cart.

9. Last _____ a storm came up at sea, and our ship was blown off course _____ the _____.

Rating   Good: 4   Excellent: 6   Ace: 8

---

30. FIGURE THIS OUT

A certain slang expression meaning "to fail" consists of a five-letter word followed by the word "out." A certain slang expression meaning "to succeed" consists of a three-letter word followed by the word "out." If you put the five-letter and three-letter words together, you will get the name of a popular book and movie for children. What is it?

31. RHYMING OPPOSITES

Provide an opposite for each word or phrase that is also that word or phrase's rhyme.

Ex. Go away _____Stay_____

1. In stature, small _____
2. Gladden _____
3. Yea _____
4. For a fee _____
5. Not yet begun _____
6. Besmear _____
7. Suffer a defeat _____
8. Like a drip _____
9. Hire _____
10. Full of vice _____
11. Where angels dwell _____
12. Ma _____
13. Feel certain about _____
14. A slew _____
15. Formal title for a her _____
16. Finishing worst _____
17. Like a prude _____
18. Think bad thoughts of _____

Rating   Good: 10   Excellent: 14   Ace: 17

---

32. BOY OH BOY!

Think of a common boy's name in seven letters. Remove the first and last letters and read the remaining five letters backward to get another common boy's name. Both are the standard full forms of their names—not nicknames. What are they?

33. LOTSA LUCK!

Every answer is a two-word name or phrase in which both words start with the letter L.

Ex. Woman who helps a bettor <u>Lady Luck</u>

1. Co-worker of Jimmy Olson and Clark Kent _____
2. Program in which kids learn baseball _____
3. Item offered by a supermarket at below cost _____
4. Star of *Mary Hartman, Mary Hartman* _____
5. She played Alice on TV's *Alice* _____
6. Movie cowboy with a 15-foot whip _____
7. Where one might hear French or Spanish tapes in school _____
8. It protects car buyers _____
9. Foppish man who frequents bars looking for women _____
10. They sink ships _____
11. Group that had the #1 hit "La Bamba" _____
12. FDR plan to help the Allies in WW2 _____
13. Undulating light fixture popular in the '60s _____
14. Author of *Last of the Breed* and *The Haunted Mesa* _____
15. Cartoon girl who was sweet on Tubby Tompkins _____

The next two answers have three words each—all starting with L.

16. Comedy by Shakespeare _____
17. Classic 1969 song by Bob Dylan _____

Finally, an answer with four words, all starting with L.

18. Classic 1966 hit by Mitch Ryder and the Detroit Wheels _____

Rating   Good: 10   Excellent: 13   Ace: 16

34. FINISHING TOUCH

There is a common three-word phrase in which all the words end in the letter F. What is it?

35. D-LETIONS

The answer to the first clue in each pair is a word with the letter D somewhere in it. Remove the D phonetically and you'll get the answer to the second clue.

Ex. President Eisenhower / Color of snow

_____Dwight_____   _____white_____

1. Huge rock / Kind of hat or sportsman

_____   _____

2. Animal with spots / Person in a colony

_____   _____

3. Long time without rain / Severe defeat

_____   _____

4. Wrote on an envelope to be mailed / Item on a police blotter

_____   _____

5. King Midas, for example / Scary film genre

_____   _____

6. Colonel in the game Clue / Something we all hope to pass

_____   _____

7. Ornaments on a necklace / Self-punishment for wrongdoing

_____   _____

8. Distance from side to side / Inhalation

_____   _____

9. Tonto, to the Lone Ranger / Person with ESP

_____   _____

10. Person who's afraid / What a person who's afraid does

_____   _____

Rating   Good: 5   Excellent: 7   Ace: 9

36. WHAT A CAD!

The letter trio C-A-D appears in the middle of a certain word. Put the same letters in front of it as you put behind it to complete a familiar new word. What is it?

_____CAD_____

37. FOLLOW-UPS

For each of the following three words, think of a fourth word that can follow it to complete a compound word or a familiar two-word phrase. Each answer has exactly three letters.

Ex. Hard	High	Old	*hat*
1. Grab	Punching	Tea	_____
2. Dragon	Fruit	Sacrifice	_____
3. Pill	Soap	Suggestion	_____
4. Black	Tongue	Windsor	_____
5. Alley	Copy	Pole	_____
6. Watch	Hot	Sheep	_____
7. Snake	Cock	Tar	_____
8. Home	Bull	Test	_____
9. Pea	Dough	Chest	_____
10. Broad	Drive	Fair	_____
11. Strong	Tone	Fire	_____
12. Water	Yule	Captain's	_____
13. Area	Oriental	Hooked	_____
14. Tight	Bitter	Dead	_____

Rating   Good: 5   Excellent: 9   Ace: 12

38. VOWEL PLAY

There's a well-known old puzzle to name a word that contains the vowels A, E, I, O, and U in order. The answer given is always FACETIOUS or ABSTEMIOUS. Can you instead think of a familiar phrase in two or more words that contains the vowels A, E, I, O, and U in order? There are many answers, but the puzzle is to think of just one.

39. TOM SWIFTIES

Fill in each blank with an adverb (ending in the suffix "-ly") to complete the sentence in a punny way. The first letter of each answer is provided as a hint.

Ex. "A's, E's, I's, O's, and U's aren't the only vowels," said Tom
   __W i s e l y__ .

1. "You woke me up to serve the navy men rum?" asked Tom
   _G_____.

2. "I'll make your Folger's coffee right away," said Tom
   _I_____.

3. "I've faced my troubles and I'll never see a psychiatrist again," said Tom _U_____.

4. "Let's get this no-good Model T started," said Tom _C_____.

5. "Hold this sign up to get the auctioneer's attention," said Tom
   _F_____.

6. "Let every lady now touch her partner," said Tom _G_____.

7. "I hereby give everyone $1,000," said Tom _G_____.

8. "Just between you and me, the corporal is about to be demoted," said Tom _P_____.

9. "My rooster can beat your rooster," said Tom _C_____.

10. "Rephrase that sentence in future perfect," said Tom _T_____.

Rating   Good: 4   Excellent: 6   Ace: 8

40. GAME EXCHANGE

Name a familiar game in four letters. Switch the order of the last two letters and you'll get the name of a completely different game. What is it? Hint: One of the games is played indoors and the other is played outdoors.

41. ESS-CAPADE

Answer each clue with a familiar word, name, or phrase that contains three consecutive S's.

Ex. Man's formal evening attire   *dress suit*

1. What Cinderella left behind at the ball   _____
2. Broadway hit set in southeast Asia   _____
3. White House spokesperson   _____
4. This might appear on kids' pants knees and is hard to remove   _____
5. Do needlework   _____
6. One of Rainier's daughters, in Monaco   _____
7. Thick slice of meat that is pounded and braised in vegetables   _____
8. It has two queens, four bishops, four rooks, 16 pawns, etc.   _____
9. What a savvy entrepreneur has   _____
10. Someone who rises from poverty to riches   _____
11. Stan Getz's instrument, only with a deeper tone   _____
12. "SOS"   _____
13. Classic surfing movie of 1966   _____
14. It's next to the judge's bench in the courtroom   _____
15. Nickname for Kentucky   _____

Rating   Good: 8   Exellent: 11   Ace: 14

---

42. APPARENT APPAREL

What two articles of apparel have names that are anagrams of each other (i.e., contain the same letters rearranged)? Hint: The items, in part, cover the same part of the body.

43. SIGN LANGUAGE

Imagine the word RESTAURANT as a large neon sign lit by individual letters. Then imagine that some of these letters are burned out, so that the remaining letters in order (but not necessarily consecutively) spell everyday words. Answer the following clues for these words.

R E S T A U R A N T

Ex. Beginning ___ S T A R T ___
[composed of the 3rd, 4th, 5th, 7th, and 10th letters, respectively]

1. Payment to a landlord _____

2. Aired again, as TV shows _____

3. *Gone with the Wind* plantation _____

4. Small pie _____

5. Talk loudly and angrily _____

6. Make, as money _____

7. It's observed from an observatory _____

8. Emanating glow _____

9. Tease cruelly _____

10. Jacob's twin, in the Bible _____

11. Brand of plastic wrap _____

12. Smallest of the litter _____

13. Going over Niagara Falls in a barrel, e.g. _____

14. Opposite of loose _____

15. Certain typewriter key _____

16. The back or end, as of an animal _____

Rating   Good: 8   Excellent: 12   Ace: 15

44. ON THE MONEY

The currency name MARK is hidden in the work REMARKABLE, and RAND is hidden in GRANDMA. What common word does DINAR appear in?

45. FALSE PLURALS

In each of the following sentences, add an S at the end of the word that goes in the first blank to get a new word that goes in the second.

Ex. Now that their rival is out of business, the local toy store plans to ___jack___ up prices on ___jacks___ and other items.

1. Though the farmer's wife had two entire bushels of corn to _____, she said, "Aw _____, that's not so bad."

2. Tomorrow I hope to _____ up with my golf buddies and spend a day at the _____.

3. It's almost _____ for people of _____ not to help the poor.

4. The English _____ wearing leather _____ fooled everyone into thinking he was a cowboy.

5. The firecracker was a _____, but the man in the fancy _____ kept trying to light it anyway.

6. Just thinking about getting honey directly from a _____ gives me the _____.

7. The supermarket _____ plays a game of _____ with the manager during her rest breaks.

8. A _____ of the soldiers moved into temporary _____, while their old barracks were being renovated.

9. The blacksmith would _____ like an elephant every time his _____ broke.

10. It was _____ that the _____ on the winning racehorses were so far off.

Rating Good: 4 Excellent: 7 Ace: 9

---

46. JUST FOR STARTERS

In the phrase "A___ and B___ the C___ of D___," the letters A, B, C, and D are the initials of the four words that will complete it. The answer is a common expression. What is it?

47. FLEXIBLE ABBREVIATIONS

Each of the following abbreviations, in everyday usage, can stand for two completely different things. What?

Ex. C.D.   *certificate of deposit*   *compact disc*

1. A.C.   _____   _____

2. P.C.   _____   _____

3. M.P.   _____   _____

4. B.C.   _____   _____

5. P.R.   _____   _____

6. O.T.   _____   _____

7. T.M.   _____   _____

8. V.J.   _____   _____

9. I.R.A.   _____   _____

10. E.R.A.   _____   _____

Rating   Good: 12 (out of 20)   Excellent: 15   Ace: 18

48. ON THE DOUBLE

Take the word SURE. If we asked you to add two pairs of doubled letters to it to make an eight-letter word, you would add P's and S's to make SUPPRESS. Can you add two pairs of doubled letters to RATE to make a common eight-letter word?

49. THE OLD ONE-TWO

Reverse the first two letters of the answer to the first clue to get the answer to the second.

Ex. '60s hairstyle / Casino card game   _Afro_   _faro_

1. Monster / Vice-President Al   _____ _____
2. Hearty brew / Rags-to-riches writer   _____ _____
3. Most unusual / Take into custody   _____ _____
4. Choice / Magical drink   _____ _____
5. County in Northern Ireland / Shine   _____ _____
6. Blue jeans / 1950s-'60s singing sensation   _____ _____
7. Shade tree / Enough   _____ _____
8. Height / Degrees from the equator   _____ _____
9. Kind of energy / Hard to understand   _____ _____
10. Storefront cover / On the way out   _____ _____
11. Beneath / Less clothed   _____ _____
12. The act of making a god / Moral improvement or guidance
  _____ _____

Rating   Good: 5   Excellent: 8   Ace: 11

---

50. FALSE COMPARISON

If the word POND were an adjective, the comparative form would be PONDER. If EARN were an adjective, the superlative form would be EARNEST. Think of a familiar four-letter word that can have either -ER or -EST added to the end to make a new word unrelated in meaning to the original. All three words are uncapitalized. Bonus hint: The original four-letter word is an informal term.

51. X TIMES TWO

Every answer here is a word, name, or familiar phrase that contains two X's.

Ex. Company founded as Standard Oil ___Exxon___

1. Woman who oversees a will _____

2. Route in an old TV series _____

3. Style of spicy cuisine _____

4. Newsboy's cry, once _____

5. Familiar interstate sign _____

6. Base line of a graph _____

7. Like income on state and local bonds, usually _____

8. Star of TV's *Sanford and Son* _____

9. Opposite of à la carte on a restaurant menu _____

10. Competitor of Serutan _____

11. Cinema with half a dozen screens _____

12. Copycat company? _____

13. 70, in French _____

14. Author of the bestseller *The Complete Book of Running*
_____

15. [Heads up!—a tricky one] 1986 event in which the Chicago Bears beat the New England Patriots _____

Rating   Good: 8   Excellent: 11   Ace: 14

---

52. URBAN PROBLEM

What major American city has the same cryptogram pattern as the word REORDER? In other words, think of the seven-letter name of an American city in which the first, fourth, and seventh letters are the same, and the second and sixth letters are the same.

53. TRICKY ANTONYMS

Provide an opposite of each of the following words, using the lengths and starting letters provided.

Ex. Minor (5 letters starting with AD)   _adult_

1. Fast (3 letters starting with EA)   _____

2. White (4 letters starting with YO)   _____

3. Out (4 letters starting with SA)   _____

4. High (5 letters starting with SO)   _____

5. Subject (5 letters starting with RU)   _____

6. Flat (5 letters starting with FI)   _____

7. Tall (7 letters starting with FA)   _____

8. Off (7 letters starting with WO)   _____

9. Rough (7 letters starting with FA)   _____

10. Odd (7 letters starting with MA)   _____

Rating   Good: 2   Excellent: 5   Ace: 8

---

54. ALL BUT ONE

Can you think of a common, uncapitalized, unhyphenated word that contains all but one of the letters of the alphabet from L to V? The missing letter is for you to determine. You may use other letters of the alphabet (before L and after V) as necessary. Our answer has 13 letters. What is it?

L M N O P Q R S T U V

55. GOING TO THE DOGS

Another visit to the Bad Pun Department. Fill in each blank with the name of a breed of dog that will complete the sentence in a punny way.

    Ex. One of the greatest natural insulators in the world is the __Wolfhound__ on a sheep's back. [wolfhound = "wool found"]

    1. Mikey takes one taste of the cod-liver oil and then _____ it out.

    2. "With this will I make you my sole _____," Roy Rogers said to his wife.

    3. When a jockey wants to make his horse run faster, generally he has to _____.

    4. Listening to the recent Congressional budget debate was enough to make you _____ hair out.

    5. "I enjoy Johann Sebastian _____," said the boy politely.

    6. Run the sail up the _____ the wind picks up again.

    7. After leaving his medical office yesterday, the _____ himself for an hour on the beach.

Finally, a really tough one:

    8. Mom just went into the bedroom. _____ nap time!

Ratings   Good: 3   Excellent: 5   Ace: 7

---

56. WITH A COMMON END

We're thinking of three words that are spelled the same except for their first two letters, which can be SW, TW, or WH. Hint: All three words have the same meaning. What are they?

57. RHYME AND REASON

Think of a synonym for each clue that is also a rhyme for it.

Ex. Shake _____quake_____

1. Glide _____
2. Whiff _____
3. Savor _____
4. Wrinkle _____
5. Wriggle _____
6. Squirm _____
7. Square _____
8. Sling _____
9. Glitch _____
10. Spy _____
11. Waver _____
12. Dot _____
13. Preacher _____
14. Clasp _____
15. Huff _____
16. Tubby _____

Ratings Good: 8 Excellent: 12 Ace: 15

---

58. NO RHYME OR REASON

Speaking of rhymes, the words RAID and SAID end in the same three letters, but they don't rhyme with each other. Can you name a third, uncapitalized word that also ends in -AID that doesn't rhyme with either of the other two?

59. SILENTS, PLEASE!

Rearrange the letters in each of the following words to get a new word that starts with a silent letter.

Ex. KEEN   K N E E

1. HANGS   _____
2. LAMPS   _____
3. TOWER   _____
4. NAKED   _____
5. ELIAS   _____
6. GROWN   _____
7. HESTON   _____
8. TRINKET   _____
9. SWELTER   _____
10. STRAITS   _____
11. DANGLER   _____
12. RELISHES   _____

Rating   Good: 5   Excellent: 8   Ace: 12

60. NEW ANSWER TO AN OLD CHALLENGE

An old puzzle asks "What word consists of two consecutive pronouns?" The answer given in all the books is USHER (i.e., US + HER). Can you think of a second answer? In the case of USHER, the first pronoun is regular and the second is possessive. In our new answer, the first pronoun is possessive and the second is regular. What is this familiar word?

61. "CH"

Every answer in this puzzle is a word, name, or phrase in which two of the syllables begin with "ch-."

Ex. Idle talk _*chitchat*_

1. Game played on a six-pointed star _____

2. Popular kind of cookie _____

3. "The Little Tramp" _____

4. Gary Kasparov or Bobby Fischer, e.g. _____

5. TV mechanism that allows you to switch stations _____

6. Comic actor once known for his imitation of Gerald Ford _____

7. He sang "The Twist" and "Let's Twist Again" _____

8. Dairy product produced in firm blocks _____

9. Fictional character with a "Number 1" son _____

10. Very quickly, in exclamations _____

11. Once-popular Dana Carvey skit on *Saturday Night Live* _____

The last three answers have "ch" three times:

12. *Mary Poppins* song sung by Julie Andrews and Dick Van Dyke _____

13. Ballroom dance, originally from Latin America _____

14. In song, it left the Pennsylvania Station about a quarter to four _____

Rating   Good: 7   Excellent: 10   Ace: 13

62. "CH$_2$"

What common six-letter word has its meaning reversed when its first letter is changed from a C to an H?

63. BACK AND FORTH

Complete each sentence with a seven-letter palindrome—a word or phrase that reads backward and forward the same.

Ex. In Norfolk, Virginia, a blue _Navy Van_ shuttles VIP's from the airport to the military base.

1. After pricing all the American-made refrigerators, John and Madge decided to get _____.

2. The Hope Diamond is so large that some newspaper writers call it a _____.

3. We traded in our old Japanese car, _____, for a new Saturn.

4. The Bushes hope to visit their old friends from Washington, the _____, during their next trip to New Hampshire.

5. According to news reports, a popular governor is angling for the _____ on the next GOP ticket.

6. The interior decorator took one look at the room and immediately decided to _____ the walls.

7. Ancient Egyptians _____ the sun and built temples in its honor.

8. When the _____ broke, the whirling stopped, and the machine would no longer work.

9. Rick Mears is testing a new _____ for the next Indianapolis 500.

Rating   Good: 4   Excellent: 6   Ace: 8

---

64. CELEBRITY ANAGRAM

You can rearrange the nine letters in the word COSTUMIER to name a famous person. Who is it? Hint: The answer consists of the celebrity's first and last names.

65. Q-TIPS

The answer to the first clue in each pair begins with the letters QU. Remove the initial "k-" sound and you'll have (phonetically) the answer to the second clue.

Ex. Duck sounds / Candle material   **quacks**   **wax**

1. Event along a fault line / Rouse from sleep   _____   _____

2. The Dionnes, e.g. / React from pain   _____   _____

3. Hush! / Gunfighter at the O.K. Corral   _____   _____

4. Musical note / Show uncertainty   _____   _____

5. Faster / Furniture material   _____   _____

6. Kind of clock / Witches have them on their noses

  _____   _____

7. Pen / These might be famous last words   _____   _____

8. Suppress / Scrub   _____   _____

9. Suppress / Source of water   _____   _____

10. Search / Pioneers' heading   _____   _____

11. Idiosyncrasy / Slave driver's command   _____   _____

12. Kind of bee / Withdraw by degrees   _____   _____

13. Kind of bee / Suffering from heat   _____   _____

14. Former Vice-President / Cry   _____   _____

Rating   Good: 8   Excellent: 11   Ace: 14

66. FIVE RINGS

The 15-letter phrase FROM BOTTOM TO TOP contains five O's and no other vowels. The 14-letter phrase FOOT-LONG HOT DOG also contains five O's and no other vowels. So does the 12-letter phrase NO ROOM TO GROW, as well as the 11-letter POOL OF BLOOD. Can you think of a common phrase in just 10 letters that contains five O's and no other vowels? Hint: There are two answers, with word lengths 6,4 and 4,2,4, respectively.

67. SWITCHING BRANDS

Change one letter in each of the following words to make a well-known brand name found at a supermarket or drugstore.

Ex. SKIMPY   *Skippy*   [peanut butter]

1. LESSON   _____
2. NESTED   _____
3. WOMBAT   _____
4. ANVIL   _____
5. SPRITZ   _____
6. BUYER   _____
7. DRANK   _____
8. PARLAY   _____
9. BENGAL   _____ (hyph.)
10. CENTS   _____
11. PLASTERS   _____
12. TWINKLES   _____
13. CAMPY   _____
14. CAMPERS   _____
15. CREPT   _____
16. FOLDERS   _____
17. RAFFLES   _____
18. BALKAN   _____ (2 wds.)
19. BASELINE   _____
20. UNISON   _____

Rating   Good: 10   Excellent: 14   Ace: 18

---

68. FOOD, GLORIOUS FOOD

The 10-letter name of something you might order at a Chinese restaurant consists of letters that all appear in the second half of the alphabet (N to Z). It is a common food with a multi-word name. What is it?

69. WATCH THAT STUTTER

Each answer in this puzzle is a phrase in which the last syllable is said three times in a row.

Ex. Muffled sounds from an African monkey *lemur murmur*

1. Isthmus mother _____

2. You can "walk the dog" with it in Japan _____

3. French dance performed by a large-billed bird _____

4. An improvised ballerina's dress _____

5. Blunder in ordering the wrong Asian furniture material?
   _____

6. Stupid bird from Denver _____

7. Driving by a New York state prison _____

8. Soft-nosed bullet for a nursery-rhyme character _____

9. What Santa says while riding to the hounds? _____

In the last answer, the final syllable appears four times in a row.

10. Humdinger in Hawaii _____

Rating   Good: 5   Excellent: 7   Ace: 9

---

70. LARGE OR SMALL

The words "Polish" and "polish" are spelled the same but have different meanings and pronunciations depending on their capitalization. With a long-O sound the word is capitalized, but with a short-O sound it isn't. Now think of two four-letter words, also spelled the same, in which capitalization has a different effect: When the word is capitalized, the first letter is pronounced, but when it's not, the first letter is silent. What are these two words?

71. DOUBLE-H

Every answer is a word, name, or phrase that contains two H's in a row.

Ex. Keep for oneself ___withhold___

1. Thumb a ride _____

2. Dressy shoes for women _____

3. Place to stick a worm _____

4. Where to change clothes at the beach _____

5. Snobbish or haughty _____

6. *Playboy* founder _____

7. *David Copperfield* character _____

8. Engage in disorderly play _____

9. Substitute for, as in the batting lineup _____

10. Participant at the Mad Hatter's tea party _____

11. Omaha or Utah, for the D-Day invaders _____

12. When traffic is the worst _____

13. Start of the Jewish New Year _____

14. Top-secret _____

15. Wild government search, as the McCarthy hearings

    _____

16. Brass wind instrument with a flared end _____

Rating Good: 9   Excellent: 12   Ace: 15

---

72. EAST MEETS WEST

In the United States most radio stations east of the Mississippi River have call letters starting with W and most stations west of the Mississippi have call letters starting with K. What common eight-letter word, with a hyphen in the middle, consists of two such radio station names—the first starting with W and the second with K? Hint: The answer is an adjective that might describe a good-looking house.

73. GOING THROUGH CHANGES

It's a common experience in crosswords: You fill an answer in the grid that, even though it fits the clue and matches a lot of the crossing letters, turns out to be wrong. Eventually, you have to change a letter to make another word that also fits the clue. This puzzle works in the same way. Change one letter in the word at the left to make a new word that just as easily fits the clue at its side.

Answer in grid	Clue	Corrected answer
Ex. AMEND	Change	E M E N D
1. STOOL	Place to sit	_____
2. PONDER	To think	_____
3. WEDDED	Joined together	_____
4. BANEFUL	Causing harm	_____
5. DEPRESS	Push down	_____
6. MILLION	Very large number	_____
7. MUDDLED	Unclear	_____
8. SCATTER	Send in all directions	_____
9. STILLED	Forced to be quiet	_____
10. STORING	Putting away for safekeeping	_____
11. WHISPER	Speak in a low voice	_____
12. WISHFUL	Longing (for)	_____
13. DROPPED	Sank	_____
14. ELASTIC	In a flexible state	_____
15. SHUNNED	Pushed aside	_____
16. JAPANESE	Asian islander	_____

Rating   Good: 10   Excellent: 13   Ace: 16

---

74. $100,000 NAME

Assign the letters of the alphabet their numerical values: A = 1, B = 2, C = 3, etc., up to Z = 26. What common first name (either male or female—that's for you to determine) has letter values that, when multiplied together, equal exactly 100,000?

75. WITHOUT ASPIRATIONS

Fill in each blank with a word starting with "wh-," which becomes a new word if the "wh-" is not aspirated (as in WHINE and WINE)—the latter of which can also go in the blank to complete the sentence. Gird yourself, because these are groaners.

Ex. I turned down the dinner invitation from the complaining vintner because I couldn't stand his ___whine/wine___.

1. A picture of the members of an early 19th-century English Parliament would show a large number of _____.

2. The bikers with the biggest Harleys _____ a lot of power.

3. If you want to know the reasons things happen, ask the

   _____.

4. The injured Pony Express rider cried "_____!" as he reined in his horse at the station.

5. Little Miss Muffet walked into the top-rated takeout shop and said "_____ to go!"

6. The Indian dervish Ajeeb entered international competition and now boasts the title "champion of the _____."

7. Confucius say: Man known for blubber spend much time

   _____.

8. When naughty Johnny didn't finish coating the kitchen floor correctly, his mother gave him extra _____.

Rating   Good: 3   Excellent: 5   Ace: 7

---

76. TELEPHONE WORD

What is the only common, uncapitalized seven-letter word in which six of the seven letters use the same number on a telephone dial? For example, the word CABBALA on a telephone would be 222-2252—but the answer is a more familiar word than that.

77. WORD ASSOCIATION

What single word can precede the three words in each of the following sets to complete a compound word or a familiar two-word phrase? Hint: Every answer is six letters long.

Ex. Control	Missile	Ship	c r u i s e
[cruise control, cruise missile, cruise ship]			
1. Goose	Oldie	Rod	_____
2. Book	Knife	Veto	_____
3. Summer	Ocean	Chief	_____
4. League	Dipper	Women	_____
5. Guess	Fiddle	Thoughts	_____
6. Band	Check	Neck	_____
7. Ages	Class	Weight	_____
8. Paint	Print	Nail	_____
9. Parlor	Sleep	Spot	_____
10. Bedroom	Mind	Plan	_____

Rating   Good: 5   Excellent: 7   Ace: 9

---

78. WORD CHAIN

The four four-letter words BOOK, MARK, DOWN, and PLAY go together, in order, to form a cyclical chain of linking compound words: BOOKMARK, MARKDOWN, DOWNPLAY, and PLAYBOOK (the last compound linking the fourth word back to the first). Can you think of four *five*-letter words that will form an equivalent chain? As in the example, the chain will take the form of 1-2, 2-3, 3-4, and 4-1. All the compounds in our answer are spelled as solid words, with the initials H, B, W, and P, respectively.

79. WHY?

Every answer is a word or name that starts with the syllable "why" (in any of its spellings).

Ex. Windshield blade ___Wiper___

1. Cheyenne's state _____

2. Bowery bum _____

3. "Stand By Your Man" singer _____

4. Pre-Hitler republic _____

5. Novelist and poet Elinor _____

6. Famous beach in Honolulu _____

7. Former Connecticut Senator and governor Lowell _____

8. Ronald Reagan's first wife _____

9. Add lanes to, as a highway _____

10. Indian tribe, or a breed of chicken _____

11. Hunting dog with a cropped tail _____

12. She played the mother on *Father Knows Best* _____

13. Two-legged winged dragon in heraldry _____

14. Painter of *Christina's World* _____

Rating   Good: 8   Excellent: 11   Ace: 13

80. IN ALPHABETICAL ORDER

The word DEGENERATIVE contains six consonants—D, G, N, R, T, and V—which are in alphabetical order reading from left to right. Can you name a major city somewhere in the world whose name also has six consonants in alphabetical order reading from left to right? The name can have only six consonants, and none can be repeated. Hint: The answer is the capital of its country.

81. INITIAL RESPONSE

Think of a member of each category here beginning with each of letters in the category's name. For example, a bird starting with B could be bobolink, buzzard, bluejay, or bullfinch. Any legitimate answer should be counted as correct.

1. B _Obolink_ _____

   I _____

   R _____

   D _____

2. F _____

   L _____

   O _____

   W _____

   E _____

   R _____

3. C _____

   O _____

   U _____

   N _____

   T _____

   R _____

   Y _____

Rating   Good: 10 (out of 16)   Excellent: 13   Ace: 16

82. WEAREVER

Take the word RIGHTNESS, add the letter O, and rearrange all the letters to name something to wear. Hint: It usually comes in pairs. What is it?

R I G H T N E S S + O = _____

83. SPOONERISMS

A spoonerism is the transposition of initial consonant sounds in a word or phrase, as in BLUSHING CROW for the expression CRUSHING BLOW. In each pair of clues below, answer the first clue to get a familiar two-word phrase that can be spoonerized to get a new two-word phrase that answers the second clue.

Ex. Precipitating hard _pouring rain_

Expressing anguish, as a lion _roaring pain_

1. Descend, as a ladder _____

   10¢ circus figure _____

2. Duel in *Zorro* or *The Three Musketeers* _____

   Where the Mustang or Taurus is made _____

3. The Constitution guarantees certain of these _____

   Kingly lamps _____

4. Crimson _____

   The correct whole wheat or pumpernickel _____

5. Post office mail receptacle _____

   Superior safeguards on a door _____

6. Ticket-holder's IOU _____

   Multiple accident on a highway _____

7. Container in which to bake a cobbler _____

   Ornament for a cravat _____

8. Brief nap _____

   Traitors with witchlike facial blemishes _____

Rating Good: 4 Excellent: 6 Ace: 8

84. MIXED NATIONALITIES

Name a certain European nationality in seven letters. Rearrange the letters in it to spell an Asian nationality. What is it? Two hints: 1) Both names start with the same letter of the alphabet. 2) The Asian nationality does not have a country of its own.

85. A LITTLE R AND R

Every answer here is a two-word proper name in which both words start with the letter R.

Ex. Girl of old song ___Rio Rita___

1. Group led by Teddy Roosevelt up San Juan Hill _____

2. Warner Bros. cartoon bird _____

3. Popular brand of beer _____

4. Popular ice cream flavor _____

5. Children's magazine published by the National Wildlife Federation _____

6. John Updike bestseller _____

7. 1943 John Wayne movie named for a tributary of the Mississippi _____

8. Nat King Cole song with the lyric "Why I love you, heaven knows" _____

9. Long-running daily TV show for preschoolers _____

10. It's between Income Tax and Oriental Avenue on a Monopoly board _____

11. Pseudonym of Leonard Slye _____

12. Mother Goose rhyme about a bird _____

13. Sir Walter Scott novel about a Scottish outlaw _____

14. Duston Hoffman role in *Midnight Cowboy* _____

15. Historic event of March 1917 _____

Rating   Good: 7   Excellent: 10   Ace: 13

---

86. CHINESE PUZZLE

If an out-of-work hairstylist is distressed, and an out-of-work political essayist is distracted, what is an out-of-work Sinologist?

87. DROPPIN' G'S

In each of the following sentences, the answer that goes in the first blank is a word ending in "-ing," minus the "g." If you have the right one, a homophone of it can go in the second blank to complete the sentence.

Ex. Dad was _muzzlin'_ the barking dog with a piece of _muslin_ cloth.

1. José was _____ Cain in the movie theater because his date wouldn't pass him a chocolate-covered _____.

2. When Sarah saw the clumsy cook _____ all the omelet orders, she order an English _____ instead.

3. Just as the thief was _____ the bank, _____ pulled up and jumped out of the Batmobile.

4. The out-of-shape ornithologist was _____ as he ran after the escaped _____.

5. Because Susan's manner of dress was _____ on Madonna's, it was hard to believe she was really an innocent _____.

6. The bathroom designer was _____ her high price on the fact that the porcelain _____ would have to be imported.

7. The seamstress' head was _____ up and down as she searched the floor for the _____ that had fallen off her sewing machine.

8. Because he was caught _____ home-made beer in his bathtub, the UCLA _____ was thrown out of his dorm.

9. The kid who was _____ down the most candy was the one dressed as a Halloween _____.

Rating   Good: 4   Excellent: 6   Ace: 8

---

88. TO SLEEP, TO SLEEP

What word meaning "stole" is composed of two successive names for places to sleep?

89. A TO Z

Each of the following words begins with the letter A. Provide a synonym starting with a Z.

Ex. Ardor   *Zeal*

1. Apex   _____

2. Absurd   _____

3. Area   _____

4. Aught   _____

5. Angling   _____

6. Automaton   _____

7. Astrological   _____

8. Animal-related   _____

9. Asleep   _____

10. Airship   _____

Rating   Good: 5   Excellent: 7   Ace: 9

90. J-Q-Z WORD SQUARE

In the word square shown below, the words BASH, AREA, SEAL, and HALT read both across and down. Can you construct a similar 4 x 4 square that uses the letters J, Q, and Z? All four words in the square must be common English words. Proper names are permitted.

```
B A S H
A R E A
S E A L
H A L T
```

91. TWO-WAY

Put two letters in each pair of dashes to complete a common, uncapitalized four-letter word that will spell another common, uncapitalized four-letter word in reverse.

Ex. A B U T   [ABUT and TUBA]

1. D _ _ W

2. G _ _ T

3. E _ _ L

4. G _ _ F

5. P _ _ G

6. B _ _ D

7. D _ _ A

8. W _ _ F

9. O _ _ E

10. D _ _ L   D _ _ L   [two answers]

11. T _ _ M   T _ _ M   [two answers]

12. E _ _ T   E _ _ T   [two answers]

Ratings   Good: 7 (out of 15)   Excellent: 11   Ace: 14

92. A LITTLE OFF THE SIDES

The word "gym" is a shortened form of the word "gymnasium," with the end chopped off. The word "bus" is a shortened form of "omnibus," with the front chopped off. Can you think of a common three-letter word that is a shortened form of a longer word in which both the front and end are chopped off? Hint: The longer word has nine letters.

93. MULTINATIONAL TANGLE

Rearrange the letters in each of the following words to name a country somewhere in the world.

Ex. ALSO   _L A O S_

1. RAIN   _____
2. PURE   _____
3. MOAN   _____
4. MAIL   _____
5. ASPIN   _____
6. PLANE   _____
7. BIALY   _____
8. LAITY   _____
9. HELIC   _____
10. CHAIN   _____
11. REIGN   _____
12. UNSAD   _____
13. ENEMY   _____
14. SERIAL   _____
15. SPRUCY   _____
16. ANALOG   _____
17. REGALIA   _____
18. ANEURISM   _____

Rating   Good: 9   Excellent: 13   Ace: 17

94. THE SILENT TREATMENT

The word PSYCHOLOGY starts with a silent P, and the word COUP ends with one. Can you name a word containing an interior silent P—and one that is not derived from French? Hint: In the answer we have in mind, the P is both preceded and followed by consonants.

95. OW!

Every answer is a word, name, or phrase, in which each of the two or more vowel sounds is "ow" (in any spelling).

Ex. Main business district of a city *downtown*

1. Indian meeting _____

2. Summer electrical power problem _____

3. It precedes a rocket liftoff _____

4. Yell louder than _____

5. Famous German school of design _____

6. Chinese breed of dog _____

7. Dog's bark _____

8. Thornton Wilder play _____

9. Vociferous person who talks too much _____

10. Discovered _____

11. Heading from Pennsylvania to Florida _____

12. High-quality hamburger _____

13. Feared African terrorists _____

14. Show servile deference (to) _____

15. Clear away snow, as from a driveway _____

16. Familiar phrase in elocution practice _____

Rating   Good: 8   Excellent: 12   Ace: 15

---

96. NAME DROPPING

Take the word BEAVER. Drop the consecutive letters V-E and you're left with BEAR—thus changing one animal name into another. The name of what animal becomes the name of another animal when you drop the consecutive letters O-N-G?

97. THE LONG AND THE SHORT OF IT

Answer the first clue of each pair with a word that has a short E sound. If you have the right one, you can change the vowel to a long E sound to get a new word that answers the second clue.

Ex. Means of payment / Part of the face _check_ _cheek_

1. Lower limb of the body / Association _____ _____

2. Estimate / Silly birds _____ _____

3. Shouted / Street sign _____ _____

4. Summon by gesture / Lighthouse light _____ _____

5. Ironed / Church official _____ _____

6. Small fruit / Slightly drunk _____ _____

7. Winter garment / More like honey _____ _____

8. A cook / Bundle of papers _____ _____

9. States / Grab _____ _____

10. Outcast / One who jumps _____ _____

11. Like some beans or crabs / Means of protection

_____ _____

12. Something on the dinnertable / Nosy person _____ _____

13. Fish / One of the five senses _____ _____

14. Numerous / Ogre _____ _____

Rating Good: 8 Excellent: 10 Ace: 13

---

98. LOW SCORE WINS

Assign every letter of the alphabet its numerical value: A = 1, B = 2, C = 3, and so on, up to Z = 26. Can you think of a familiar 11-letter word whose letter values total only 39?

99. HINKY-PINKY

Answer each one-word clue with a two-word rhyming phrase. Answer lengths are provided in parentheses.

Ex. Electrocardiogram (5,5) _heart chart_

1. Crawl (2,4) _____
2. Soar (3,4) _____
3. Olympus (5,4) _____
4. Chardonnay (4,4) _____
5. Ton (5,6) _____
6. Beacon (6,5) _____
7. Tennis (5,5) _____
8. Coma (4,5) _____
9. Mammogram (6,4) _____
10. Tide (5,6) _____

Rating   Good: 4   Excellent: 7   Ace: 9

---

100. INSIDE TRACK

A certain seven-letter word starts with the letter R and ends with the letter E. Inside are two words that are opposites of each other, one after the other. What is the full word?

R_____E

101. WOULD YOU REPEAT THAT?

Every answer is a four-word phrase in which the first and third words are the same.

Ex. Incessantly

___ *Day in, day out* ___

1. Expression that means "Everything's fine up to this point"

_____

2. Slogan for an election in which everyone has an equal voice

_____

3. Phrase said by someone who is spending money too freely

_____

4. Motto for someone who's working out strenuously at the gym

_____

5. Expression about a chip off the old block

_____

6. Home of Rutgers University

_____

7. Start of Santa's call to his reindeer

_____

8. Jocular saying by a worker about his pay as he goes home at night

_____

9. Using any available means or method

_____

10. Start of a children's rhyme about wishing at night

_____

11. 1983 James Bond movie starring Sean Connery

_____

12. Common policy on order of accepting orders

_____

13. Phrase about imitation, said in reference to primates

_____

14. Circus barker's call outside a tent

_____

Rating   Good: 7   Excellent: 10   Ace: 13

---

102. GAG!

What two rhyming words are both synonyms of "gag"—in two different senses?

103. THE COMMON TOUCH

What word identifies what each of the following sets of three things have in common?

Ex. Barber   Rooster   Beehive
_____*Combs*_____

1. Bowling alley   New shirt   Wrestling match
_____

2. Pelican   Legislature   Person with a charge card
_____

3. Telephone   Toy chest   Car trunk
_____

4. Parking lot   Olympic swimming pool   Electric company
_____

5. Car transmission   Lady's wardrobe   Night watchman
_____

6. Bird   Theater stage   Decorated pilot
_____

7. Golfer   Laundry room   Dungeon
_____

8. Tennis tournament   Cigarette machine   Twins
_____

9. Fishing rod   Actor   Checkout counter
_____

10. Deck of cards   Beehive   New York City
_____

Rating   Good: 4   Excellent: 7   Ace: 9

---

104. ON THE CONTRARY

Rearrange the 11 letters in the phrase SHOUT "DANGER!" to make two words that are opposites of each other. What are they? The words can have six and five letters, respectively, or seven and four letters, etc.—the lengths are for you to determine.

105. UP A TREE

Another visit to the Bad Pun Department. Put the name of a tree in each blank to complete the sentence in a punny way.

Ex. To see how to operate a fax machine, watch me _C y p r e s s_ the "start" button. [cypress = "as I press"]

1. After scoring the winning soccer goal, Sally became the most _____ girl in school.

2. If Virgil loses this poker hand, he _____ us 50 more dollars.

3. With this much studying to do before tomorrow's exam, I _____ an all-nighter.

4. As soon as the rodeo pony started to _____ fell off.

5. From a very early age Bobby Fischer could be described as a _____.

6. There has never been, for patients who are really _____ useful medicine.

7. If Jerry takes the car into the city with you, make _____ the doors.

8. After the big office screwup, we knew the boss would _____ poor slob out.

9. In preparation for possible suicide, Cleopatra kept an _____ a small box.

10. The President had dinner at our house once, and that's the very _____ sat in.

11. Between the air pollution that stings your eyes and the air pollution that affects your breathing, _____ bother you more? [2 wds.]

12. Thanks, mom. Whenever our photos appeared in the newspaper, _____ out.

Rating Good: 5   Excellent: 8   Ace: 11

---

106. DOWNSIZING

From what word can you drop the last four letters without affecting the pronunciation?

107. FOR FATHER'S DAY

Every answer in this puzzle is a word, name, or phrase that starts with the syllable "tie" (in any spelling).

Ex. Angry speech ___*tirade*___

1. Neighbor of Laos _____
2. River through Rome _____
3. River through Baghdad _____
4. Final stage of a contest _____
5. President before Polk _____
6. Business magnate _____
7. Bufferin or Anacin competitor _____
8. Means of self-defense _____
9. New Testament book after II Timothy _____
10. Herman Melville novel _____
11. Detroit baseballer _____
12. Storm in the western Pacific _____
13. Popular toilet cleaner _____
14. Historic fort in the American Revolution _____
15. Secretary, often _____
16. Heavyweight champ who KO'd Spinks _____
17. Boxing championship _____
18. Oppressive dictator _____
19. A country . . . _____
20. . . . and its capital _____

Rating   Good: 12   Excellent: 16   Ace: 19

---

108. MIDDLEWEIGHT

If we asked "The name of what famous person phonetically contains the word TURKEY?"—you would say Buster Keaton ("bus-TURKEY-ton"). Now tell us: The name of what famous person phonetically contains the word KILO?

109. CHANGE OF COLOR

Change one letter in each word to name a color.

Ex.	WED	R E D
1.	BLUR	_____
2.	GOOD	_____
3.	PINE	_____
4.	TRAY	_____
5.	RUBS	_____
6.	EMBER	_____
7.	BLOWN	_____
8.	MORAL	_____
9.	GREED	_____
10.	OTHER	_____
11.	ALIVE	_____
12.	ROUGH	_____
13.	BRONTE	_____
14.	SHERRY	_____
15.	GRANGE	_____
16.	VIENNA	_____
17.	BELLOW	_____
18.	STARLET	_____

Rating   Good: 14   Excellent: 16   Ace: 18

110. CHANGE OF SHOE

Name an informal kind of shoe in two syllables. Then phonetically reverse the two syllables to get a word meaning "leave of absence." What are the two words?

111. B AND B

Every answer is a word, name, or phrase that starts and ends with the letter B.

Ex. Spill the beans _____blab_____

1. Lobster eater's protection _____

2. Police officer's stick _____

3. Writing on a book jacket _____

4. Stinging remark _____

5. Criticize in an underhanded way _____

6. Start for a tulip _____

7. Another name for the Devil _____

8. Tiniest bit left over from a sandwich _____

9. Item with a ring _____

10. Simpleton _____

11. Thick-trunked African tree _____

12. Smear all over _____

13. Search for seashells, for example _____

14. Grizzly's baby _____

15. What you might run up before dinner at a restaurant

_____

Rating   Good: 10   Excellent: 12   Ace: 14

---

112. GOING BACK ON ONE'S WORD

What word meaning "imposed on another's generosity" contains seven letters in reverse alphabetical order—with no letters repeated?

Z Y X W V U T S R Q P O N M L K J I H G F E D C B A

113. PAST-TIME

Put the same word in both blanks to complete each sentence. Every answer is a word ending in "-ed" that has two meanings.

Ex. Georgette _pointed_ at the boy who had made the _pointed_ remark about her shoes.

1. We _____ the kegs of beer onto the truck, because the owner was too _____ to do it himself.

2. The TV producers _____ the employee who added _____ laughter to the sitcom.

3. The argyle socks the seamstress _____ now look _____ impressive.

4. Before the inspector distributed her "Inspected by #23" stickers, she _____ every black-and-white _____ shirt inside and out.

5. Everyone knew that the man in the _____ suit would be _____ in the arm-wrestling contest.

6. Dad was so mad he _____ the salesman who had sold him used _____ tires.

7. The enemy commander looked _____ in the face after our troops _____ his men out of the woods.

8. The game that Greg Maddux _____ turned out to be a _____ battle between rival teams.

Rating Good: 3 Excellent: 5 Ace: 7

114. CAPITAL TIME

A two-part challenge: a) The first four letters of which U.S. state capital spell the name of a month? b) The first *six* letters of which U.S. state capital also spell a month?

115. N.G.

Each answer here is a familiar two-syllable word, name, or phrase in which each syllable ends in the letters "-ng."

Ex. Upset, as nerves _jangling_

1. Game played in a rec room _____

2. Having a monotonous rhythm, as a nursery rhyme _____

3. New York state prison _____

4. Big party _____

5. Capital of North Korea _____

6. Awkwardly tall and spindly _____

7. Sound of a doorbell _____

8. Rock group with the 1986 hit "Everybody Have Fun Tonight"
_____

9. 1966 Cher hit, or the sound of a gun _____

10. Hero of Pearl Buck's *The Good Earth* _____

11. Asian stock exchange site _____

12. Beautiful girl, after the word "sweet" _____

13. Big name in circuses _____

14. Famous movie with a scene at the Empire State Building
_____

15. [2 answers:] Washington Zoo pandas, given to the United States by China in 1973 _____ _____

Rating Good: 8 (out of 16)   Excellent: 11   Ace: 13

---

116. EXTRA SOFT

A "hard G" is the letter G as it is pronounced in the word GAME. A "soft G" is a G as it is pronounced in GIANT. Name a common six-letter word—uncapitalized and unhyphenated—that contains two soft G's.

117. TWO FOR TWO

The following are some seven-letter words and the clues that might appear for them in a crossword. For each one, change two *consecutive* letters in the word to get a new word that would also answer the clue.

Ex.	FOUNDRY	Place of manual labor	L A U N D R Y
1.	LUGGAGE	Suitcases	_____
2.	CALCIUM	Chemical element	_____
3.	CONTEND	Compete	_____
4.	CURRENT	Flow	_____
5.	LUNATIC	Crazy person	_____
6.	MAXIMUM	Extreme amount	_____
7.	SPARKLE	Glitter	_____
8.	EVASIVE	Difficult to pin down	_____
9.	GRIPPED	Seized	_____
10.	SHIVERY	Tremorous	_____

Rating   Good: 5   Excellent: 7   Ace: 9

---

118. REPEATING NUMBER

The number NINE contains the letter N twice. Change both N's to P's and you get the word PIPE. What is the next number above nine that you can do this to? In other words, what is the next spelled-out number that has a repeated letter that can be changed to the same new letter in both places to make a familiar new word? Hint: The new letter will not repeat any other letter in the word.

119. "A" PUZZLE

In each three-word answer to this puzzle, one of the words is the article "a" followed by another word. Join the "a" and the following word phonetically and you'll get the third word—which may either begin or end the phrase.

Ex. Have the money for an American car Afford a Ford

1. Bide one's time for a scale reading _____

2. A brassy woman overseas _____

3. Concerning a boxing match _____

4. Approximately three minutes in a boxing match _____

5. A flower sprang up _____

6. Fights a government levy _____

7. Slightly leading, as in a horserace _____

8. A superior partner in crime _____

9. A sound is bothersome _____

10. Gain workers for a ship _____

11. A nun's helpers _____

12. Get a large amount of paper _____

13. A competitor's appearances _____

14. Mom or dad in plain view _____

Rating   Good: 7   Excellent: 10   Ace: 13

120. MYSTERY BOOK

A man was in a library and spotted an interesting-looking book on a shelf. Its spine read "HOW TO JOG." Upon opening the book he found that it was not a manual on running. In fact, the book had nothing to do with jogging in any sense of the term. What kind of book was it?

121. BLANK OF THE BLANK

Every answer is a familiar four-word phrase or title in which the middle two words are "of the" and the first word starts with the letter L. Note: Some of the answers consisting of titles have an additional "The" at the start.

Ex. Person often asked for in a home sales call *lady of the house*

1. Plant with bell-shaped flowers _____

2. James Fenimore Cooper novel _____

3. A strict judge follows it _____

4. Person who's lots of fun on social occasions _____

5. Tolkien trilogy _____

6. Sir Walter Scott poem _____

7. Terrain _____

8. Part of the last line of "The Star-Spangled Banner" _____

9. "Only the strongest survive" _____

10. A matter of chance, in cards _____

11. William Golding novel _____

12. Body of water between Minnesota, Manitoba, and Ontario _____

13. There are 26 of them _____

14. 1964 #1 hit for the Shangri-Las _____

Rating Good: 6 Excellent: 9 Ace: 12

122. ON THE UP AND UP

There are seven consonants in our alphabet that, when written in small letters, have ascenders—b, d, f, h, k, l, and t. Can you think of a common word that contains six of these seven consonants, once each, and no other consonants? (You may add vowels as necessary.) Hint: The answer is a hyphenated adjective that does not describe anyone who solves this puzzle.

123. SOUNDING PRESIDENTIAL

Still another puzzle from the Bad Pun Department. In each sentence, put the name of a U.S. President in the blank to complete the sentence in a punny way.

Ex. The doctor made me drink some foul-tasting ___Madison___.

1. Buck Rogers whipped out his _____ and shot the alien.

2. The man thought his wife was cheating on him, so he hired a detective to _____.

3. _____ any doctors in the house?

4. I'm havin' trouble _____ these cars together on the train.

5. A good bartender should be able to _____ than two glasses at a time.

6. The Celtics got to shoot a technical foul in New York's Madison Square Garden because there were six _____ the floor.

7. The woman from Boston _____ dress on a nail.

8. I didn't believe in love at first sight, but then I looked into her _____ hearts beat as one.

Rating   Good: 3   Excellent: 5   Ace: 7

---

124. IT MIGHT AS WELL BE GREEK

Can you put two Greek letters together phonetically to form a common, hyphenated English word? Without the hyphenation requirement, you might have joined "pi" and "rho" to make PYRO, or "chi" and "rho" to make CAIRO. But the answer is hyphenated, and it uses the English-language pronunciation of the letters, not the Greek. What word is it?

125. FOOD FOR THOUGHT

For each of the following foods, provide a familiar proverb or saying (not just a phrase or expression) that contains the food name somewhere within it. Answers may not be unique.

Ex. Bread   _Man doth not live by bread alone_

1. Eggs   _____

2. Milk   _____

3. Meat   _____

4. Apple   _____

5. Honey   _____

6. Broth   _____

7. Omelet   _____

8. Sauce   _____

9. Fish   _____

Finally, three dessert items . . .

10. Cookie _____

11. Cake   _____

12. Pudding _____

Rating   Good: 4   Excellent: 6   Ace: 9

---

126. YOU SAID A MOUTHFUL

What is the only one common, uncapitalized, seven-letter English word, containing just a single vowel—that does *not* have the letter S anywhere within it? Hint: The answer starts with T.

127. 2-D

Every answer in this puzzle is a two-word phrase or name in which each word begins with the letter D.

Ex. See a movie as a foursome, perhaps *double-date*

1. First two words of an entry in a personal journal _____

2. Transaction that's final _____

3. 1967 film about 12 World War II prisoners, with *The*
   _____

4. Make a long-distance call without operator assistance
   _____

5. Where to stick a floppy _____

6. Sultry part of summer _____

7. Basketball no-no _____

8. Brand of minivac _____

9. 1973 #1 hit for Helen Reddy _____

10. Huey, Dewey, and Louie's uncle _____

11. Villainous sailor in *H.M.S. Pinafore* _____

12. 1967 Rex Harrison film role _____

13. One who avoids military service _____

14. Place for ship repair _____

15. Batman and Robin, with "the" _____

16. 1983 movie with Jennifer Grey and Patrick Swayze
    _____

17. Fancily-dressed guy _____

18. Something contestants bet on in *Jeopardy!* _____

Rating   Good: 8   Excellent: 12   Ace: 16

128. COLLEGE MEN

The name of what annual college event contains the letter sequence M-E-N twice?

129. BROOKLYNESE

Longtime residents of Brooklyn are famous (at least in myth) for pronouncing their "words" like "woids." That is, the "ur" sound comes out as "oi." Sometimes this change produces an entirely new word. Answer each of the following pairs of clues with two words that are pronounced the same except that the first contains an "ur" sound where the second has "oi." (Spelling may vary.)

Ex. Snarling dog / Bashful
_____*c u r*_____   _____*c o y*_____

1. Throw / Noted authority on games
_____   _____

2. Famous duelist / Lad
_____   _____

3. Poetry / Something a singer has
_____   _____

4. Sounds of contentment / Self-assurance
_____   _____

5. Get an education / Butcher's cut
_____   _____

6. Famous newspaper publisher / Lift
_____   _____

7. Roll up / Wrapping paper
_____   _____

8. In the lead / Impose by fraud or trickery
_____   _____

9. In the wee hours / Greasy
_____   _____

10. Stated / Shun
_____   _____

Rating   Good: 5   Excellent: 7   Ace: 9

---

130. BROOKLYNESE 2

As a followup puzzle, what word and its Brooklynese counterpart are synonyms of each other? That is, what two words with the same meaning are also pronounced the same except that one has an "ur" sound where the other has "oi"? Hint: Both words are four letters long.

131. X MARKS THE SPOT

Fill in the blanks in each sentence with two homophones—words that are pronounced the same but spelled differently. Hint: The first word of each pair ends in the letter X.

Ex. In ferrying across the river **Styx**, Charon **sticks** his pole in the water.

1. Not laughing at a _____ Brothers movie _____ a person as pretty humorless.

2. Sales _____ is something a merchant _____ onto the price.

3. Since my little brother worked at the refreshment stand, I tried to _____ him into giving us free _____.

4. Whenever the weightlifter would _____ his muscles especially hard, _____ of dandruff fell from his head.

5. George reserved a _____ seat to hear _____ Brandenburg Concertos.

6. After another poor basketball season, New Yorkers said _____ to the _____.

7. A child who grows up under _____ rules often _____ a sense of responsibility.

8. In *Jurassic Park*, T. _____ angrily _____ the museum.

9. In fields full of marigolds and _____, Alice saw whole _____ of birds.

10. At Fort _____, guards must learn via the school of hard _____.

11. As the leader of the jazz band, the _____ player sometimes _____ another member of the group.

12. When the rodeo came to New York City, residents of the _____ saw bucking _____ close up for the first time.

Rating   Good: 5   Excellent: 8   Ace: 11

---

132. GOING BUGGY

If you add the letter G to the name of a certain insect and rearrange all the letters, you can get the name of a different insect. What two insects are they?

133. MIND YOUR P'S AND Q'S

Each answer in this puzzle is a word, name, or phrase that starts with the letter P and contains a Q somewhere within it. Answer lengths are provided in parentheses.

Ex. Resentment (5) _____pique_____

1. Award that hangs on the wall (6) _____

2. Ahab's ship in Moby Dick (6) _____

3. Fancy floor woodwork (7) _____

4. Agreeably stimulating (7) _____

5. *Butch and Sundance: The Early Days*, e.g. (7) _____

6. Unexpected test (3,4) _____

7. Bodybuilder's form (8) _____

8. Herbicide used to kill marijuana (8) _____

9. Insignificant person (9) _____

10. Bonus or right that comes with a job (10) _____

11. Nearness in time or place (11) _____

12. Having natural beauty, as a scene (11) _____

Rating Good: 5 Excellent: 8 Ace: 11

---

134. NUMBER, PLEASE

If you say the number "ten" after the letter B, you get the word BEATEN. What three numbers other than ten can phonetically follow a B (spoken as "be") to complete other common English words?

BE_____   BE_____   BE_____

135. END TO END

Every answer is a five-letter word or phrase in which the first two letters are the same as the last two letters in the same order.

Ex. Taste or touch, for example ___*Sense*___

1. The Lone Ranger's faithful friend _____

2. Car from Sweden _____

3. Molten rock under the earth's surface _____

4. Sen. Kefauver, Adlai Stevenson's 1956 running mate

   _____

5. Florida city named for an Indian tribe _____

6. It can bring a tear to your eye _____

7. Author Franz, of *Metamorphosis* _____

8. Making a great noise, as a crowd _____

9. Walked sideways in itty-bitty steps _____

10. Personal enthusiasm or vigor _____

11. Up, in baseball (2 wds.) _____

12. Slang for yes (hyph.) _____

13. Derek and the Dominos hit of 1972 _____

14. One of the conspirators against Caesar _____

15. Lively Latin-American music _____

Rating   Good: 8   Excellent: 11   Ace: 14

136. SPANISH INQUISITION

Think of a common male Hispanic first name in four letters. Put it inside a common female Hispanic first name in five letters to get a common nine-letter English word. What is it?

137. THE NAME OF THE GAME

Complete the following story by putting the name of a familiar game in each blank.

What rotten luck! Aaron had a flat tire in the car (ex.) _p o o l_ lane on the single-span (1)_____ just outside of town. He wished some passing motorists would offer him their (2)_____, because he didn't have one. Officer Bentley stopped to help. Unfortunately, Aaron had been drinking, because his breath smelled (3)_____, and the out-of-date (4)_____ on the back of his car showed that his registration had expired. Oops! Bentley proceeded to ask Aaron more than (5)_____—his date of birth, mother's maiden name, etc.—as a sobriety test. Then he phoned headquarters, where his various (6)_____ found that Aaron had a long record of drunken driving. The enraged Aaron began to (7)_____ with the officer and threaten him with a (8)_____ from the fireplace set he was taking home. But Aaron didn't have a (9)_____ of a chance. "Sorry, Aaron," Bentley said, disarming the man. "You'll have to (10)_____ to jail!"

Rating Good: 3 Excellent: 5 Ace: 8

---

138. MEMPHIS

The 13-letter word METAMORPHOSIS contains all the letters of MEMPHIS at least once. The 11-letter word MIMEOGRAPHS does, too. So does the 10-letter MEMBERSHIP. Can you think of a word in just nine letters that contains all the letters of MEMPHIS?

139. TO DO

Every answer here is a two-syllable word, name, or phrase in which each syllable ends in the sound "oo." The spelling of the "oo" sound varies.

Ex. Sound of crying _boohoo_

1. Crazy, or a kind of clock _____
2. Black magic, informally _____
3. South African tribesman _____
4. Nobel Prize–winning bishop _____
5. Popular chocolate soft drink _____
6. Toy train _____
7. Completely loyal _____
8. Blunder _____
9. Dress worn by Hawaiian women _____
10. She sang the 1967 hit "To Sir with Love" _____
11. Kind of eyes that lovers make _____
12. Burmese Prime Minister of the '40s, '50s, and '60s _____
13. Kind of platter at a Polynesian restaurant _____
14. Put down as insignificant _____
15. Popular rock group led by Bono _____
16. *Star Trek* role played by George Takei _____

Rating   Good: 8   Excellent: 11   Ace: 14

---

140. MUSIC THEORY

Fill in the following blank with a two-word phrase containing a total of seven letters: _____ music. Change the last letter of your answer to a new letter and you can fill in the following blank with another two-word phrase of seven letters: _____ theory. What words go in the blanks?

141. TWO BY TWO

For each of the following five-letter words, provide another word *starting with the same two letters* that can follow it to complete a compound word or a familiar two-word phrase.

	Ex. PIZZA	*pie*
1.	SWORD	_____
2.	SHELL	_____
3.	MATCH	_____
4.	HOBBY	_____
5.	ROUND	_____
6.	FLASH	_____
7.	MARSH	_____
8.	SEVEN	_____
9.	SHARP	_____
10.	TABLE	_____
11.	INDIA	_____
12.	TUMMY	_____
13.	SHORT	_____
14.	WHOLE	_____
15.	STAND	_____
16.	CABLE	_____
17.	MAGIC	_____

In the final answers, the first *three* letters are repeated.

18.	CANDY	_____
19.	TRAIN	_____
20.	SPOIL	_____

Rating   Good: 10   Excellent: 14   Ace: 18

142. GUYS

Rearrange the letters in the word PERPETUAL to form two boys' names—one in five letters and one in four. What are they?

143. O BOY!

Answer each clue with a word, name, or phrase that has somewhere within it an O followed by an apostrophe.

Ex. Halloween pumpkin _jack-o'-lantern_

1. Cap with a wide, round, flat top _____

2. Phosphorescent light seen over a marsh _____

3. Noon _____

4. Brand of butter _____

5. Cause of the great Chicago Fire, according to legend

_____

6. America's busiest airport _____

7. Nasty whip _____

8. Famous racehorse upset by Upset _____

9. Having a triangular shape, as dress sleeves _____

10. #1 Elvis hit of 1959 _____

11. In song, a girl "sweeter than the rose of Erin" _____

12. Brand of coffee _____

13. Very tiny person _____

14. Greeting at the start of the day _____

Rating   Good: 6   Excellent: 9   Ace: 12

144. O, NO!

The word AROUND is often shortened by removing the initial A, as in "round-the-clock" or "round the fireside." Can you think of a word that is often shortened by removing the initial O?

145. END ALIKE

Each answer is a pair of five-letter words that end in the same three letters and have the same definition.

Ex. Kind of tree   M a p l e   a p p l e

 1. Another kind of tree   _____   _____

 2. Look steadily (at)   _____   _____

 3. Tiny spot   _____   _____

 4. Behindhand   _____   _____

 5. Tremble   _____   _____

 6. Give instruction to   _____   _____

 7. Hit with the open hand _____   _____

 8. Dance   _____   _____

Rating Good: 3   Excellent: 5   Ace: 6

---

146. NOVEL WORD LADDER

This challenge is a variation on the old game of word ladders. The list below shows how to turn SHREW into TIMID by successively changing one letter at a time and making a new word at each step.

```
S   H   R   E   W
S   H   R   E   D
S   I   R   E   D
T   I   R   E   D
T   I   M   E   D
T   I   M   I   D
```

In these five steps the word SHREW has been turned into a new word in which the letters in all five positions are different from what they were at the start. Can you do the same with SMITE—in five steps turn it into a new word in which the letters in all five positions are new? Plurals and verbs formed by adding S are not allowed. All your steps must be common, uncapitalized English words.

147. FOR YOUR I'S ONLY

Fill in the first blank in each sentence with a word that has a short I sound. If you have the right one, you can change the vowel to a long I sound to get a new word that goes in the second blank to complete the sentence.

Ex. Sometimes watching the cabin stewards __flit__ from seat to seat is the best part of the airplane __flight__.

1. According to the brothers _____, Cinderella had to clean the _____ from the fireplace while her stepsisters went to the ball.

2. It was overcast during our entire week in Great _____, and skies didn't _____ till we got to France.

3. Advice to Hell's Angels members: No matter how much you may disagree with him, never _____ with another _____.

4. No matter how much the fashion industry tries to bring it back, the miniskirt is _____ out of _____.

5. The big _____ at the zoo was throwing his weight around so wildly, we had to give him a _____ to calm him down.

6. The crowd outside the jewelry shop _____ the police when they learned the law enforcers were too late to stop the diamond _____.

7. Between the blond _____ on the back of his head and the _____ way he chomped on his gum, Dennis the Menace was constantly embarrassing his mother.

8. The laundryman had to use a _____ full of bleach to get the stain out of the baby's _____.

9. I knew the sales clerk was a bit of a _____ when she falsely claimed the _____ used in making the blouse was real silk.

10. The hammer and _____ are no longer part of the Russian flag now that the _____ of Communism is over.

Rating   Good: 5   Excellent: 7   Ace: 9

148. BODY PARTS

Name two parts of the body that are pluralized not by adding an S to their names, but by changing their vowels.

149. RHYMING TRIOS

Think of rhymes for each trio of words that will go together to make a familiar phrase in the form "___, ___, and ___."

Ex.	Plop	Shook	Christen	*Stop, look, and listen*
1.	Frappe	Cackle	Strop	
2.	Brook	Sign	Thinker	
3.	Bread	Height	Drew	
4.	Done	June	Chars	
5.	Freddie	Chilling	Stable	
6.	Claim	Fret	Scratch	
7.	Dreg	Sorrow	Wheel	
8.	Shuns	Blitz	Terrors	
9.	Drop	Whip	Thump	
10.	Bomb	Quick	Marry	
11.	Rock	Rock	Carol	
12.	Crawl	Shark	Ransom	
13.	Mud	Threat	Dears	
14.	Quell	Nook	Scandal	
15.	Teddy	Fame	Shire	
16.	Wraith	Scope	Clarity	
17.	Skin	Mace	Throw	
18.	Through	Strut	Chair	

Ratings   Good: 12   Excellent: 15   Ace: 18

---

150. AUTHOR! AUTHOR!

Take the last name of a well-known American writer. Insert the letter P and you'll get the last name of a well-known British writer. Who are these two authors?

151. A DAY AT THE BEACH

Every answer here is a word or name that contains the syllable TAN.

Ex. Peelable fruit *tangerine*

1. Brightly colored songbird _____

2. Tree-dwelling ape _____

3. Seaport of Morocco, on the Strait of Gibraltar _____

4. Ill-fated ship of 1912 _____

5. Bicycle built for two _____

6. Wickerwork material _____

7. Its nickname is Big Sky Country _____

8. Popular carol about a Christmas tree _____

9. Mideast robe _____

10. Seven-piece Chinese puzzle _____

11. Tease by overpromising _____

12. Small seedless raisin _____

13. Opera by Wagner _____

14. Card game also called parliament or sevens _____

15. Its capital is Dar-es-Salaam _____

16. Fiendishly cruel (like this puzzle?) _____

Rating   Good: 10   Excellent: 12   Ace: 14

152. TWO-TONE

Name a common English word that contains the consecutive letter combination T-A-N-T-A-N.

153. BRAVING THE ELEMENTS

Anagram each of the following words and letters to get the name of an element on the periodic table.

Ex. LOG + D =   _GOLD_

1. LEVIS + R =   _____
2. FURLS + U =   _____
3. RANG + O =   _____
4. RUMBA + I =   _____
5. ACORN + B =   _____
6. CLINK + E =   _____
7. BLOAT + C =   _____
8. MUSIC + E =   _____
9. CRANES + I =   _____
10. MERINO + B =   _____
11. SUBMIT+ H =   _____
12. NUPTIAL + M =   _____
13. RENTING + O =   _____
14. MISTUTOR + N =   _____

Rating   Good: 6   Excellent: 10   Ace: 14

---

154. PSEUDO-OPPOSITES

The words SHOT and SCOLD are pseudo-opposites because SHOT is S + HOT and SCOLD is S + COLD. Can you think of two pseudo-opposites that end in the letter T (i.e., two words ending in T that become antonyms when you remove the T's)? Hint: One of the answer words has five letters and the other has three (before the T's are removed).

155. DIS-INFORMATION

Yes, another visit to the Bad Pun Department. Complete the blank in each of the following sentences with a word starting with the prefix "dis-" that completes the sentence in a punny way. "Dis-" always equals "this" in the pun. As a bonus hint, a definition of the "dis-" word appears somewhere in the sentence.

    Ex. Please take apart <u>dismantle</u> from over the fireplace.
        [dismantle = "this mantel"; defined in the sentence as "take apart"]

1. _____ seems to look with scorn on his native Copenhagen.

2. When the orchestra played _____, the result was a cacophonous combination of notes.

3. _____ was filled with alarm by the mess the butler left her to clean up.

4. I managed to convince Elvis by argument not to use _____ for his blue shoes.

5. _____ was thrown out of the Shakespearean poets' club.

6. Firing _____ at the terrorists' base will break up their evil operation.

7. We decided to take the money from _____ we found on the street and scatter it about.

8. One who argues with me a lot said, "_____ plate is not as pretty as the bronze one."

9. The perfume tester said, "I do not agree with the majority! _____ stinks!"

Rating   Good: 3   Excellent: 5   Ace: 7

---

156. OVERLAPPING STATES

The word MARINE consists of five consecutive, overlapping state postal abbreviations—Massachusetts (MA), Arkansas (AR), Rhode Island (RI), Indiana (IN), and Nebraska (NE). Can you think of a common seven-letter word that has the same property? Hint: The first letter is also M.

157. HOW IN-TERESTING

Insert the word IN in each of the following words (at the start, at the end, or somewhere inside) to get a new word.

Ex. ROUTE   R O U T I N E

1. PATER   _____
2. IMAGE   _____
3. MUTES   _____
4. VILLA   _____
5. SWISH   _____
6. SPIRE   _____
7. BASSET   _____
8. MISTER   _____
9. CLARET   _____
10. BULLET   _____
11. MILLER   _____
12. FATNESS   _____
13. CONTENT   _____
14. BRALESS   _____
15. FANCIER   _____

Rating   Good: 13   Excellent: 14   Ace: 15

---

158. BASEBALL GEAR

Think of a word for an article of clothing worn below the waist. Then think of a word for an article of clothing worn above the waist. Put them together, without rearranging letters, and you'll get a word used in baseball. What is it?

159. WE GET LETTERS

Every answer is a word that begins with a letter of the alphabet followed by a hyphen. Hint: No beginning letter will be repeated in the puzzle.

Ex. Casual garment *T-shirt*

1. Ski lodge shape, often _____

2. Brand of roach killer _____

3. Striptease garment _____

4. WW2 Army food _____

5. Revealing dress design _____

6. Very revealing picture? _____

7. Cotton swabs for the ear _____

8. Camera lens setting _____

9. Seldom-played song on a 45 r.p.m. _____

10. Construction support in a skyscraper _____

11. Upright line in a graph _____

12. Powerful nuclear weapon _____

13. National supplier of trucks and vans _____

14. Computer-to-computer communications _____

15. Faulty rocket part in the *Challenger* disaster _____

16. $100 bill _____

Rating   Good: 9   Excellent: 12   Ace: 15

---

160. SCRIPT TEASE

When you're writing in script, there are four letters of the alphabet that can't be completed in one stroke—"i" and "j" (which require dots) and "t" and "x" (which require crosses). Can you think of a common English word that uses each of these letters exactly once?

161. SHIFTY

In each of the following pairs, shift the last letter of the first answer to the next letter of the alphabet to get the second answer.

Ex. Prize / Conscious
    award aware

1. Frighten / Winter apparel worn around the neck
   _____ _____

2. Person who poses for pictures / Computer-telephone link
   _____ _____

3. Having a surface that's curved outward, as a lens / Transport
   _____ _____

4. Adherent to Islam / Cotton fabric
   _____ _____

5. Distance used in astronomy / Analyzed grammatically
   _____ _____

6. Very fine, as a cigar / Groom oneself in front of a mirror
   _____ _____

7. 31st President of the United States / Horses' feet
   _____ _____

8. County north of San Francisco / Auto racer Andretti
   _____ _____

9. Sound of a wheel that needs greasing / Sound of a pig that's being greased
   _____ _____

10. Extremely ugly / Thieves' getaway spot
    _____ _____

Rating   Good: 5   Excellent: 7   Ace: 9

162. SALTY LANGUAGE

There are four common words in the English language that contain the consecutive letters N-A-C-L. Name any three of them.

163. ONE OR THE OTHER

For each of the following familiar two-word phrases, provide a third word that rhymes with one of the words in the phrase and means the opposite of the other. The antonym and rhyme may be in either order.

Ex. In doubt   _____Out_____
[opposite of "in" and a rhyme for "doubt"]

1. Black light   _____

2. No less   _____

3. Rail pass   _____

4. Short haul   _____

5. Plain crazy   _____

6. All rise!   _____

7. Common share   _____

8. Went straight   _____

9. Fresh trail   _____

10. Wild game   _____

11. Work day   _____

12. Straight A   _____

Rating   Good: 6   Excellent: 9   Ace: 12

164. CRYPTO-GEOGRAPHY

The name of what well-known geographical location in the United States has the same cryptogram pattern as the word BEDRESSED? Thus, the nine-letter answer will have the second, fifth, and eighth letters the same; the third and ninth letters the same; and the sixth and seventh letters the same. Bonus hint: The answer has no letters in common with BEDRESSED.

165. BE VERY QUIET!

Every answer here is a word or name that contains the sound "sh" twice.

Ex. Tell to be quiet ___s h u s h___

1. Embarrassed or bashful _____

2. Form of marijuana _____

3. Potpourri _____

4. Indian tribe of the Far West _____

5. In good order, nautically speaking _____

6. Crack gunsman _____

7. Oyster, e.g. _____

8. Wisconsin city on Lake Winnebago _____

9. Cook food on a skewer _____

10. Bootblack's work _____

11. Indecisive, or without strong character _____

12. Former county of western England, the setting for an A.E. Housman volume _____

13. Mean-spirited, as a woman _____

14. Top-secret _____

Rating   Good: 7   Excellent: 10   Ace: 13

---

166. A CHANGE OF CLOTHES

Name an article of clothing in five letters. Change the second letter to a new letter to get the name of another article of clothing. Then change the fourth letter of that word to a new letter to get the name of a third article of clothing. What are the three words?

167. FORE AND AFT

Answer each clue with a word that starts and ends with the same three letters in the same order.

    Ex. Establishing oneself in the good graces of _ingratiating_

    1. Win in a yelling contest _____

    2. London's subway, with "the" _____

    3. Puts back in its original condition _____

    4. Process of becoming electrically charged _____

    5. Impressively successful person, as a lawyer _____

    6. Movies, music, comedy, magic, etc. _____

    7. Ban or Mitchum, e.g. _____

    8. Person who makes photocopies _____

    9. Capable of being washed with Clorox _____

    10. One who is teasingly cruel _____

    11. Found, as a lost city _____

    12. Ladies, in French _____

Rating   Good: 5   Excellent: 8   Ace: 10

168. FORE AND AFT 2

As a followup puzzle, can you name a famous person (living or dead) whose eight-letter last name also starts and ends with the same three letters in the same order? Hint: The first letter is a vowel.

169. CATEGORIES FOR SUMMER

Think of an answer for each category below beginning with each of the letters B-E-A-C-H. For example, if the category were "Girls' names," you might say *Betty, Ethel, Alice, Connie,* and *Heather.* Fill in one answer per box. Your answers do not have to match ours.

	ITEMS OF FURNITURE	U.S. PRESIDENTS	BASKETBALL TERMS	* CURRENT MAKES OF CARS	CABLE TV CHANNELS
B					
E					
A					
C					
H					

*makes, *not* models.

Rating   Good: 14   Excellent: 19   Ace: 24

170. FOUR-LETTER WORDS

The name of what famous work of literature consists of five four-letter words?

171. SPORTS TALK

What common term, in two different senses, is used in each of the following pairs of sports or games? The answers' first letters are provided as hints.

Ex.	Auto racing	Golf	Driver
1.	Baseball	Bowling	S_____
2.	Golf	Badminton	B_____
3.	Football	Fishing	T_____
4.	Golf	Poker	C_____
5.	Tennis	Swimming	S_____
6.	Ice hockey	Chess	C_____
7.	Karate	Tennis	C_____
8.	Weightlifting	Basketball	P_____
9.	Sailing	Poker	D_____
10.	Horseracing	Billiards	S_____
11.	Bridge	Baseball	G_____
			[2-word answer]

Finally, think of a term common to all three of these sports:

12.	Wrestling	Bowling	Golf	P_____

Rating   Good: 5   Excellent: 8   Ace: 11

---

172. A HARD ONE

The name of a certain metal consists of the names of two animals, reading in order from left to right, one after the other. The first animal name has four letters and the second has three. What metal is it?

173. SAME OLD SAME OLD

Fill in the blanks in each sentence with two words that are spelled the same but have different pronunciations and meanings.

Ex. The magician with the ___bow___ tie took a deep ___bow___ after his performance.

1. You need to _____ your _____ a little more before you speak to Lech Walesa.

2. "For your own _____, please don't drink any more _____, Mr. Takashone."

3. If the marathoner wants to regain his _____, he'll have to get the _____ out.

4. The _____ workers in Teamsters local 761 found that the metallic compound was _____.

5. If you _____ along the newly blacktopped road, your shoes might get _____.

6. The nurse _____ a strip of cloth around the injured man's _____.

7. It'll take me a _____ or two to get this _____ splinter out of your hand.

8. Joan Collins could _____ all the young men with her grand _____ into the ballroom.

Ratings   Good: 4   Excellent: 6   Ace: 8

---

174. JUST DO IT

Name three four-letter words starting with D-O that are mutual synonyms.

DO____   DO____   DO____

175. Q–Z QUIZ

Every answer in this puzzle is a word, name, or phrase that contains the two rarest letters in the English language—Q and Z.

Ex. Trivia test ____*quiz*____

1. Rock that sparkles _____

2. Bed cover made of random patches _____

3. English monarch beginning in 1952 _____

4. Hug _____

5. Make sedate _____

6. Card game related to pinochle _____

7. Area around a hospital, to traffic _____

8. Dave Brubeck group, for example _____

9. 1968 hit by Creedence Clearwater Revival _____

10. French for 14 _____

11. Former capital of the Philippines _____

12. Edward Woodward detective series on '80s TV, with *The*
_____

13. Feathered serpent god of the Aztecs _____

14. Iraqi Deputy Prime Minister, a special envoy before the Gulf War
_____

15. Neighbor of Zimbabwe _____

16. In mattresses, it's larger than full _____

Rating   Good: 7   Excellent: 10   Ace: 14

---

176. ON VACATION

Rearrange the letters of the word ADORABLY to spell the name of an annual event. What is it?

177. CHEAT SHEET

Answer the first clue in each pair with a word starting with CH. Change the CH to an SH sound and phonetically you'll get the answer to the second clue.

Ex. Select / What you wear on your feet
<u>c h o o s e</u>   <u>s h o e s</u>

1. Part of the face / Part of the leg
_____ _____

2. Another part of the face / Very stylish
_____ _____

3. Inexpensive / Followers
_____ _____

4. Cough drop flavor / Variety of wine
_____ _____

5. Kind of cheese / One that casts off
_____ _____

6. Time period in a polo match / One that casts off
_____ _____

7. Blackened, as fireplace logs / Fragment, as of earthenware
_____ _____

8. Refrigerate / Person in a con game
_____ _____

9. Leader of an Indian tribe / Bundle of papers
_____ _____

10. Leader of a meeting, in modern talk / Percentage
_____ _____

11. Gossip / Break into many pieces
_____ _____

12. In an upbeat mood / UPS, for example
_____ _____

Rating   Good: 5   Excellent: 8   Ace: 11

178. FOUR-"N"-ER

What familiar eight-letter word contains four N's—and no other consonants?

179. INDIAN CORN

One final visit to the Bad Pun Department. Insert the name of a native American tribe in each blank to complete the sentence in a punny way.

Ex. After 50 years of weeding vegetables, I hope I __Navajo__ another row of beans in my life.

1. Did you see the Three Stooges episode where Larry, Curly, and _____ newspapers on the street?

2. George gets out of prison today, and this time I _____ goes straight.

3. The chessplayer knew he was about to have a piece captured, but that wasn't the lowly _____ expected to lose.

4. Perry Mason wonders — what will his secretary _____ to the trial?

5. After it had been mended one too many times, the farmer would no longer wear such _____ pair of overalls.

6. Shakespeare's Hathaway was so bashful that we might refer to her as _____.

7. The groveling visitor bowed to the savant. "_____," he said, "thou art all-wise."

8. The detective declared the stains on the rocking _____ to solving the crime.

Rating   Good: 3   Excellent: 5   Ace: 7

---

180. FOREIGN FOOD

Name a European city in nine letters in which four of the letters are the same. Drop all four of these repeated letters, and the remaining five letters, in order, will spell something that most people like to eat. What is it?

181. THREEBIES

Every answer in this puzzle is a word, name, or phrase, in which each syllable begins with the letter B. Hint: Each answer has at least three syllables.

Ex. Yellow-and-black insect *bumblebee*

1. Louisville slugger, for example _____

2. Period beginning in 1946, population-wise _____

3. The South and Midwest, religiously speaking _____

4. Like some commentary, in boxing matches _____

5. Star of *My Favorite Martian* and *The Incredible Hulk* _____

6. Luxurious way to unwind _____

7. Rival of Denny's and Howard Johnson's _____

8. Singer/record producer married to Whitney Houston _____

9. Yogi's sidekick, in the cartoons _____

10. When a parent tucks a child into bed, words that complete the phrase "Don't let the . . ." _____

11. Paul Newman's eyes, for example _____

12. In small increments _____

13. Thorny shrub _____

The last answer has four syllables, all starting with B:

14. 1926 song whose chorus begins: "Pack up all my care and woe, here I go singing low . . ." _____

Rating   Good: 6   Excellent: 10   Ace: 13

---

182. LETTER BANK

The 12-letter name of what occupation consists of the letters S-E-U-R-A-T (repeated as necessary), and no others?

183. INTERNAL BODY PARTS

What is the shortest familiar word that contains the names of each of the following body parts? Each answer must have at least one letter before and after the body part's name. Capitalized words, plurals, verbs formed by adding "-s," and past tense forms are not allowed. The numbers in parentheses indicate the total number of letters that need to be added. Some names may have more than one answer.

Ex. _____C_____ HAIR _M A N_ (4)

1. _____ EAR _____ (2)

2. _____ LEG _____ (2)

3. _____ CHIN _____ (2)

4. _____ RIB _____ (2)

5. _____ ARM _____ (2)

6. _____ LIPS _____ (3)

7. _____ LIVER _____ (3)

8. _____ GUM _____ (3)

9. _____ HEEL _____ (3)

10. _____ NAPE _____ (3)

11. _____ SHIN _____ (3)

12. _____ ANKLE _____ (4)

13. _____ CHEST _____ (4)

14. _____ NOSE _____ (6)

Rating Good: 7 Excellent: 10 Ace: 13

---

184. PRESIDENTIAL COUSINS

Take the last name of a certain U.S. President. Change one letter to a new letter. Then rearrange all the letters to get the last name of another U.S. President. Who are these two men?

185. FALSE RHYMES

Each answer here is a two-word phrase in which the two words look like they should rhyme, but don't.

Ex. Not as good a nag _Worse horse_

1. Desires trousers _____

2. Grizzly that's trailing all the others _____

3. Slightly wet marsh _____

4. Tremendous danger _____

5. Circular injury _____

6. Rugged tree branch _____

7. One who measures the quality of H_2O _____

8. Highly unusual ditch-digger's tool _____

9. Adult Ronald McDonald _____

10. Striped jungle cat from a West African country
_____

11. Ceasar's wife, for example _____

12. Greatest amount of frozen dew _____

13. Chilled fabric from sheep _____

14. Girl dressed in a Scottish pattern _____

15. Which person's proboscis? _____

Rating   Good: 7   Excellent: 11   Ace: 14

---

186. MAKE MINE A DOUBLE

Name two containers for alcoholic beverages. Put one after the other and you'll get a common phrase that has nothing to do with alcohol. What is it?

187. SEX-CHANGE OPERATIONS

Answer each pair of clues with two words that are identical except for their first letters, which are F and M, respectively.

Ex. Dentist's handiwork / Walking around, as at a party

filling   _milling_

1. Football booboo / Speak indistinctly
   _____ _____

2. Instrument at a hoedown / Center
   _____ _____

3. Incite, as a rebellion / Short period of time
   _____ _____

4. Sink or bathtub, for instance / Blend
   _____ _____

5. Scientific achievement of 1939 / Military aim
   _____ _____

6. Like some breakfast cereals / Highly embarrassed
   _____ _____

7. A large one is a sign of intelligence / State university in Kentucky
   _____ _____

8. Declare illegal / Kind of humor
   _____ _____

9. Place to find coins / Huge pile
   _____ _____

10. The end / '60s dresses
    _____ _____

Rating   Good: 5   Excellent: 7   Ace: 9

---

188. MALE AND FEMALE

While we're on the subject of gender—a word for a male hog plus a word for a female deer, when pronounced together one after the other, sound like the name of a variety of wine. What is it?

189. A CERTAIN MYSTIQUE

Every answer in this puzzle is a word or name that ends in the letters "-que."

Ex. Unlike any other __Unique__

1. Ornate style of architecture, music, or art _____

2. Striptease stage show _____

3. Dance club _____

4. Small, exclusive group of friends _____

5. It may be on your teeth or the dentist's wall _____

6. Noted cubist Georges _____

7. Old and collectable _____

8. Ayatollah's place of worship _____

9. Not transparent _____

10. Very ugly, as a deformed face _____

11. Slanting, or at an angle _____

12. Native of northern Spain _____

13. Country between Tanzania and South Africa _____

14. Game played with 128 cards _____

15. Iowa city, home of Clarke College _____

16. French island in the Caribbean _____

17. Small clothing shop _____

18. Force that produces rotation in an engine _____

19. Thick, creamy soup _____

20. Off-color, as a joke _____

Rating   Good: 10   Excellent: 15   Ace: 19

190. DIVIDE TO UNITE

Think of a word that means "unite." Insert the letter L somewhere within it and you'll get a new word that also means "unite." What are the words?

191. AFTER-WORDS

What word can follow the three words in each of the following sets to complete a trio of compound words or familiar two-word phrases? Hint: Every answer has seven letters.

Ex. American   Orient   Pony   **Express**
[American Express, Orient Express, Pony Express]

1. Pin   Sofa   Whoopie   _____
2. Sewing   Adding   Pinball   _____
3. Liquid   Tape   Counter   _____
4. Building   Oedipus   Inferiority   _____
5. Circuit   Heart   Ice   _____
6. Train   Radio   Filling   _____
7. Speed   Lip   Palm   _____
8. Hasty   Plum   Rice   _____
9. Surgeon   Secretary   Lieutenant   _____
10. Safe   Soda   Fire   _____
11. Traffic   Thought   Remote   _____
12. Fraternity   Soul   Oh   _____

Rating   Good: 4   Excellent: 7   Ace: 10

---

192. HIDDEN OPPOSITES

Consider the word GASOLINE. You can rearrange its letters to spell GAIN and LOSE, which are mutual opposites. Two questions: a) What two opposites can you find in the word SPEARLIKE? And b) What two opposites can you find in THEOLOGIST?

193. SOLVING WITH E'S

Fill in the first blank in each sentence with a word that has a doubled E. If you have the right one, you can drop one of these E's to get a new word that goes in the second blank to complete the sentence.

Ex. At the Israeli kibbutz, the largest _*Seeder*_ broke down just two days before the _*Seder*_.

1. Shortly before her last movie, actress Meryl _____ came down with _____ throat.

2. If the teacher finds another marijuana _____ in your desk, she will _____ you to the principal's office.

3. What has the _____ _____ with the gift he received?

4. Maria has decided on a lifetime _____ as a _____ of handicapped children.

5. Searching for further incriminating evidence, the police decided to _____ the apartment of the _____, who was their prime suspect.

6. At the annual car dealers' _____, managers were _____ out praise for their best salespeople.

7. The _____ on Fred's leg, which he got near the hive yesterday, prevented him from _____ his record at the track meet. [Note: The first answer is a two-word phrase.]

8. Despite a fierce struggle for control, the soldier failed to _____ the Jeep driven by the enemy military _____.

Rating Good: 3 Excellent: 5 Ace: 7

194. SPORTING CHANCE

Name a certain sport. Take the first three letters in its name and reverse them, and you'll get an article of equipment used in the sport. What sport is it?

195. TEEN PROBLEM

Every answer is a word or name that ends in the syllable "teen" (in any spelling).

Ex. Kind of monk or monastery _Benedictine_

1. Singer known as "The Boss" _____

2. Isolation to prevent the spread of disease _____

3. Brand of chewing gum, good for after meals _____

4. Addictive substance in cigarettes _____

5. Hiker's water container _____

6. The Pope's chapel at the Vatican _____

7. Nutritionally, what meat is full of _____

8. From Buenos Aires, for example _____

9. Absolutely spotless _____

10. How Marie Antoinette lost her head _____

11. Customary procedure _____

12. Brand of antiseptic spray for soothing sunburns _____

13. Cracker with lots of little holes _____

14. Popular chocolate malt drink _____

15. Black-and-white dairy animal _____

16. With "beta," a source of vitamin A _____

17. Prepared with spinach, in cookery _____

18. Saint for whom a Florida city is named _____

Rating   Good: 10   Excellent: 14   Ace: 17

196. MAKINGS OF A WRITER

Take the word DRAGLINES, add the letter J, and rearrange all the letters to name a famous writer. Who is it?

197. FINE FUN

Answer each clue with a two-syllable word in which both syllables start with F.

Ex. Lightning bug *firefly*

1. Sound of trumpets _____
2. Give up, as rights _____
3. Relating to McDonald's or Burger King _____
4. Carry out, as an obligation _____
5. Parachutist's state, upon bailing out _____
6. Bare-knuckled boxing match _____
7. Widely dispersed _____
8. Police officer, in slang _____
9. Trick or deception _____
10. Sudden reversal of policy _____
11. Quadrupled _____
12. Stop motion, in TV or movies _____
13. Vanguard _____
14. Blunder in serving in tennis _____
15. Compel to eat _____
16. Outlandish or hard to believe _____

Rating   Good: 8   Excellent: 12   Ace: 15

---

198. APOSTROPHIZING

The word "jack-o'-lantern" contains an apostrophe and two hyphens. Can you think of another word containing one apostrophe and two hyphens in which the apostrophe does not follow the letter O? Hint: The answer is a common 10-letter word that's in every standard dictionary.

199. END GAME

Answer each pair of clues with two six-letter words that are the same except that their last two letters are switched.

Ex. Declares untrue / Girl's name
    D E N I E S   D E N I S E

1. Not thickly settled / Bowling scores
   _____ _____

2. Baseball's Mickey / Projection over a fireplace
   _____ _____

3. Stately dance / Extremely small
   _____ _____

4. Opening between slats / Famous museum
   _____ _____

5. Kind of oil / World leader who assumed power in 1959
   _____ _____

6. Picasso, for one / Biblical measures of length
   _____ _____

7. Land that a king rules / Italian for "tomorrow"
   _____ _____

8. Quit / Serenade again
   _____ _____

9. Popular card game / Well-known newspaper publisher
   _____ _____

10. Robin Hood's sweetheart / Where a yacht docks
   _____ _____

11. High-pitched scream / Bird with a hooked bill
   _____ _____

12. Goes hunting, like a cat / Chocolate dessert
   _____ _____

Rating   Good: 6   Excellent: 9   Ace: 11

---

200. TH- TH- TH- THAT'S ALL FOLKS!

What common six-letter word contains a silent TH?

ANSWERS

1. BODY LANGUAGE
1. Veto (V + toe)
2. O'Hare (O + hair)
3. Decaf (D + calf)
4. Winos (Y + nose)
5. Deliver (D + liver)
6. Oleg (O + leg)
7. Teach-in (T + chin)
8. Pinochle (P + knuckle)
9. Begum (B + gum)
10. Excise (X + eyes)

2. GOING AROUND IN CIRCLES
Possible answers include: doodad, pagoda, booboo, and baobab (an African tree).
A less familiar answer: ogdoad (a group of eight divine beings).
A hyphenated answer: do-good.

3. PLAY IT BY EAR
1. Cricket
2. Poker
3. Hockey
4. Bowling
5. Chess
6. Soccer
7. Bridge
8. Judo (or in England, Cluedo)
9. Bingo
10. Polo
11. Squash
12. Caroms
13. Boccie
14. Croquet
15. Snooker
16. Luge
17. Wrestling
18. Darts and hearts

4. NUT CASE
Pecan to tiger

5. YOU CAN SAY THAT AGAIN
1. Ate eight
2. Sail sale
3. Patients' patience
4. Horse hoarse
5. Aloud allowed
6. Ceiling sealing
7. Leased least
8. New gnu knew
9. To two, too
10. Wright write right

6. TO THE REAR
Eat (ate)

7. "SIR!"
1. Circus
2. Sirloin
3. (Rod) Serling
4. Surname
5. Circle
6. *Serpico*
7. Survey
8. Circe
9. Certiorari
10. Serbian
11. Surprise!
12. Service
13. Circumflex
14. Surgery
15. Serpent
16. Syrup
17. Surrogate
18. Cerberus
19. Serkin
20. Sermon

8. "I" ON AMERICA
Connect-i-cut

9. SHIFTING INTO REVERSE

1. Avid diva
2. Devil lived
3. Sleek keels
4. Remit timer
5. Stroh's shorts
6. Made Edam
7. Okie's Seiko
8. Repel leper
9. Laid dial
10. Dennis sinned
11. Pupil's slip-up
12. Knits stink
13. Faced decaf
14. Redips spider
15. Stressed desserts

10. ANIMALS BACKING UP

Tackle (elk and cat)

11. TWO-IN-ONE

1. Commerce
2. Excelled
3. Pollster
4. Primmest
5. Steering
6. Accurate
7. Tattooer
8. Needless
9. Bullying or buddying
10. Dismally

12. COINING NAMES

We found 10 answers, as follows:
Front
Bert, Ty (in "Liberty"); Tru (in "In God We Trust")
Back
Ned, Ed (in "One Dime"); Ted (in "United");
Tate (in "States"); Eric, Ric (in "America");
Uri (in "Pluribus").

13. S & S

1. Sticks and stones
2. Stars and Stripes
3. *Sanford and Son*
4. Searches and seizures
5. Slow and steady
6. Soup and sandwich or soup and salad

7. Simon and Schuster
8. Scratch and sniff
9. Stage and screen
10. *Summer and Smoke*
11. Scotch and soda
12. Sea and Ski
13. Spick and span
14. Sweet and sour

14. S & S, TOO

Blossom to bloom

15. ANIMALISTIC

1. Jackal (jack'll)
2. Alpaca (I'll pack a)
3. Gorilla (girl of)
4. Reindeer (rain, dear)
5. Porcupine (pork you pine)
6. Wildebeest (willed a beast)
7. Bison (bye, son)
8. Panda (panned a)
9. Cheetah (cheater)
10. Gopher (go for)
11. Woodchuck (would chuck)
12. Antelope (aunt elope)

16. ANIMAL HEAD

Fox to ox

17. PUZZLE WITH AP-PEAL

1. Isabella
2. Bellhop or bellboy/bellgirl
3. Clarabell
4. Belly button
5. Saul Bellow
6. Belleau Wood
7. Belles-lettres
8. Bluebell
9. Pot-belly stove
10. Bellicose or belligerent
11. Rubella
12. *The Bell Jar*
13. Portobello Road
14. Belladonna
15. Bellwether
16. Melvin Belli
17. Bell-bottoms
18. Ralph Bellamy

18. IT'S ELEMENTARY
Basic and sick bay

19. MUMBO-JUMBO
1. Comb
2. Stamp
3. Straw
4. Penny
5. Button
6. Nail file
7. Eraser
8. Index cards
9. Needle
10. Key

20. YOU DON'T SAY!
Yacht

21. TWO G'S
1. Gaggle
2. Go-go
3. (Paul) Gauguin
4. Goggles
5. Googol
6. Gorgon
7. Gurgle
8. Gewgaw or geegaw
9. Geiger
10. Genghis
11. (John) Gielgud
12. Goo-goo
13. Gaga
14. (Nikolai) Gogol
15. Gangling or gangly
16. Giggle
17. Gargoyle
18. Groggy

22. HEAVY THOUGHTS
Propound, program, and proton

23. NAME SCRAMBLE
1. Elsa
2. Enid
3. Dawn
4. Olga
5. Grace
6. Lydia
7. Betsy
8. Rhoda
9. Evelyn
10. Melissa
11. Darlene
12. Loretta
13. Desiree
14. Tabitha
15. Caroline
16. Marianne or Annmarie
17. Isabella
18. Rosalind
19. Catherine
20. Geraldine

24. PEN AND INK
Open and oink

25. CATEGORIES
Possible answers are shown below. Your answers may differ.
U.S. States A—Alabama, Alaska, Arizona, Arkansas; P—Pennsylvania; R—Rhode Island; I—Idaho, Illinois, Indiana, Iowa; L—Louisiana
Things in a Kitchen A—apron; P—paring knife, peeler, pots, pans; R—range, refrigerator, ricer, rotisserie; I—icebox, ice maker; L—linoleum, ladle
Parts of a Car A—axle, accelerator, alternator, antenna, air conditioner, ashtray; P—piston, plugs, pedal, pressure gauge; R—radiator, radio, roof, runningboard, rearview mirror; I—ignition, interior light; L—locks, lights, lug nuts, license plate
Units of Measure A—angstrom, acre; P—pound, peck, pint, point (in typesetting), parsec; R—rod, rad, ream, roentgen; I—inch; L—league, liter, light-year, long ton
Books of the Bible A—Amos, Acts; P—Psalms, Proverbs, Philemon, Peter I and II; R—Ruth, Romans, Revelation; I—Isaiah; L—Leviticus, Lamentations, Luke

26. IN A JAM
Pickle

27. OXYMORONS
1. Bottom top
2. Noisy (or loud) still
3. Evens odds
4. Slow fast
5. Pretty ugly
6. Specific general
7. Few lots
8. Square hip
9. Swell shrink
10. Bar permit
11. Sharp flat
12. Hidden plain

28. CARNIVAL SIGN
GROTESQUE

29. FOR THE BIRDS
1. Spar + row
2. Part + Ridge
3. Chic + Ken
4. Spoon + bill
5. Par + rot
6. Pig + eon
7. Nut + cracker
8. Whip + poor + will
9. Night + in + gale

30. FIGURE THIS OUT
Peter Pan (peter out, pan out)

31. RHYMING OPPOSITES
1. Tall
2. Sadden or madden
3. Nay
4. Free
5. Done
6. Clear
7. Beat
8. Hip
9. Fire
10. Nice
11. Hell
12. Pa

13. Doubt
14. Few
15. Sir
16. First
17. Lewd or nude
18. Love

32. BOY OH BOY!
Gregory and Roger

33. LOTSA LUCK!
1. Lois Lane
2. Little League
3. Loss leader
4. Louise Lasser
5. Linda Lavin
6. Lash LaRue
7. Language lab
8. Lemon law
9. Lounge lizard
10. Loose lips
11. Los Lobos
12. Lend-Lease
13. Lava lamp
14. Louis L'Amour
15. Little Lulu
16. *Love's Labour's Lost*
17. "Lay Lady Lay"
18. "Little Latin Lupe Lu"

34. FINISHING TOUCH
Chief of staff

35. D-LETIONS
1. Boulder, bowler
2. Leopard, leper
3. Drought, rout
4. Addressed, arrest
5. Hoarder, horror
6. Mustard, muster
7. Pendants, penance
8. Breadth, breath
9. Sidekick, psychic
10. Coward, cower

36. WHAT A CAD!
Abracadabra

37. FOLLOW-UPS
1. Bag
2. Fly
3. Box
4. Tie
5. Cat
6. Dog
7. Pit
8. Run
9. Nut
10. Way
11. Arm
12. Log
13. Rug
14. End

38. VOWEL PLAY
Possible answers: Lawn tennis court, battle it out, have it out, half serious, place in doubt, trade discount, and wandering soul. Your answer may differ.

39. TOM SWIFTIES
1. Groggily
2. Instantly
3. Unshrinkingly
4. Crankily
5. Forbiddingly
6. Gently
7. Grandly
8. Privately
9. Cockily
10. Tensely

40. GAME EXCHANGE
Pool and polo

41. ESS-CAPADE
1. Glass slipper
2. *Miss Saigon*
3. Press secretary
4. Grass stain
5. Cross-stitch

6. Princess Stephanie
7. Swiss steak
8. Chess set
9. Business sense
10. Success story
11. Bass saxophone
12. Distress signal
13. *Endless Summer*
14. Witness stand
15. Bluegrass State

42. APPARENT APPAREL
Shoe and hose

43. SIGN LANGUAGE
1. Rent
2. Reran
3. Tara
4. Tart
5. Rant
6. Earn
7. Star
8. Aura
9. Taunt
10. Esau
11. Saran
12. Runt
13. Stunt
14. Taut
15. Return
16. Rear

44. ON THE MONEY
Ordinary

45. FALSE PLURALS
1. Shuck, shucks
2. Link, links
3. Mean, means
4. Chap, chaps
5. Dud, duds
6. Hive, hives
7. Checker, checkers
8. Quarter, quarters
9. Bellow, bellows
10. Odd, odds

46. JUST FOR STARTERS
Above and beyond the call of duty

47. FLEXIBLE ABBREVIATIONS
1. Air conditioning,
   alternating current
2. Personal computer,
   politically correct
3. Military police,
   Member of Parliament
4. Before Christ,
   British Columbia
5. Public relations,
   Puerto Rico
6. Overtime,
   Old Testament
7. Trademark,
   transcendental meditation
8. Video jockey,
   victory over Japan
9. Irish Republican Army,
   individual retirement account
10. Earned run average,
    Equal Rights Amendment

48. ON THE DOUBLE
Roommate

49. THE OLD ONE-TWO
1. Ogre, Gore
2. Lager, Alger
3. Rarest, arrest
4. Option, potion
5. Ulster, luster
6. Levi's, Elvis
7. Maple, ample
8. Altitude, latitude
9. Nuclear, unclear
10. Awning, waning
11. Under, nuder
12. Deification, edification

50. FALSE COMPARISON
Temp, temper, tempest

51. X TIMES TWO
1. Executrix
2. Sixty-six
3. Tex-Mex
4. Extra, extra!
5. Next exit
6. X-axis
7. Tax-exempt
8. Redd Foxx
9. Prix fixe
10. Ex-lax
11. Sixplex
12. Xerox
13. *Soixante-dix*
14. James Fixx
15. Super Bowl XX

52. URBAN PROBLEM
Atlanta

53. TRICKY ANTONYMS
1. Eat
2. Yolk
3. Safe
4. Sober
5. Ruler
6. Fizzy
7. Factual
8. Working
9. Fairway
10. Matched

54. ALL BUT ONE
Ventriloquism

55. GOING TO THE DOGS
1. Spitz (spits)
2. Airedale (heir, Dale)
3. Whippet (whip it)
4. Terrier (tear your)
5. Boxer (Bach, sir)
6. Mastiff (mast if)
7. Dachshund (doc sunned)
8. Schnauzer (Shh! Now's her)

56. WITH A COMMON END
Swirl, twirl, and whirl

57. RHYME AND REASON
1. Slide
2. Sniff
3. Flavor
4. Crinkle
5. Wiggle
6. Worm
7. Fair
8. Fling
9. Hitch
10. Eye or pry
11. Quaver
12. Spot
13. Teacher
14. Grasp or hasp
15. Puff
16. Chubby

58. NO RHYME OR REASON
Plaid

59. SILENTS, PLEASE!
1. Gnash
2. Psalm
3. Wrote
4. Knead
5. Aisle
6. Wrong
7. Honest
8. Knitter
9. Wrestle
10. Tsarist
11. Gnarled
12. Heirless

60. NEW ANSWER TO AN OLD CHALLENGE
Thy-me

61. "CH"
1. Chinese checkers
2. Chocolate chip
3. Charlie Chaplin
4. Chess champion
5. Channel changer
6. Chevy Chase
7. Chubby Checker
8. Cheddar cheese
9. Charlie Chan
10. Chop-chop
11. "Church Chat"
12. "Chim-Chim-Cheree"
13. Cha-cha-cha
14. Chattanooga Choo Choo

62. "CH_2"
Comely to homely

63. BACK AND FORTH
1. An Amana
2. Megagem
3. A Toyota
4. Sununus
5. Top spot
6. Repaper
7. Deified
8. Rotator
9. Racecar

64. CELEBRITY ANAGRAM
Tom Cruise

65. Q-TIPS
1. Quake, wake
2. Quints, wince
3. Quiet, Wyatt
4. Quaver, waver
5. Quicker, wicker
6. Quartz, warts
7. Quill, will
8. Quash, wash
9. Quell, well
10. Quest, west
11. Quirk, work
12. Queen, wean
13. Quilting, wilting
14. Quayle, wail

66. FIVE RINGS
Voodoo doll and door to door

67. SWITCHING BRANDS
1. Wesson (cooking oil)
2. Nestea (tea)
3. Combat (insecticide)
4. Advil (analgesic)
5. Sprite (soft drink)
6. Bayer (aspirin)
7. Drano (drain cleaner)
8. Parkay (margarine)
9. Ben-Gay (analgesic)
10. Certs (breath mints)
11. Planters (peanuts)
12. Twinkies (snack cakes)
13. Camay (soap)
14. Pampers (disposable diapers)
15. Crest (toothpaste)
16. Folger's (coffee)
17. Ruffles (potato chips)
18. Kal Kan (pet foods)
19. Vaseline (petroleum jelly)
20. Unisom (sleeping tablets)

68. FOOD, GLORIOUS FOOD
Wonton soup

69. WATCH THAT STUTTER
1. Panama mama
2. Tokyo yo-yo
3. Toucan cancan
4. Impromptu tutu
5. Bamboo boo-boo
6. Colorado dodo
7. Passing Sing Sing
8. Tweedledum dumdum
9. Tally-ho ho ho!
10. Honolulu lulu

70. LARGE OR SMALL
Herb and herb

71. DOUBLE-H
1. Hitchhike
2. High heels
3. Fishhook
4. Bathhouse
5. High-hat
6. Hugh Hefner
7. Uriah Heep
8. Roughhouse
9. Pinch-hit
10. March Hare
11. Beachhead
12. Rush hour
13. Rosh Hashana
14. Hush-hush
15. Witch hunt
16. French horn

72. EAST MEETS WEST
Well-kept

73. GOING THROUGH CHANGES
1. Stoop
2. Wonder
3. Welded
4. Baleful
5. Repress
6. Billion or zillion
7. Muddied or fuddled
8. Spatter
9. Stifled
10. Stowing
11. Whimper
12. Wistful
13. Drooped
14. Plastic
15. Shunted
16. Javanese

74. $100,000 NAME
Betty
Other words that multiply to
100,000 are tee-hee and Beatty.

75. WITHOUT ASPIRATIONS
1. Whigs/wigs
2. Wheeled/wield
3. Whys/wise
4. Whoa/woe
5. Whey/way
6. Whirled/world
7. Whaling/wailing
8. Whacks/wax

76. TELEPHONE WORD
Monsoon (666-7666)

77. WORD ASSOCIATION
1. Golden
2. Pocket
3. Indian
4. Little
5. Second
6. Rubber
7. Middle
8. Finger
9. Beauty
10. Master

78. WORD CHAIN
Housebreak, breakwater, waterpower, and powerhouse

79. WHY?
1. Wyoming
2. Wino
3. (Tammy) Wynette
4. Weimar
5. Wylie
6. Waikiki
7. Weicker
8. (Jane) Wyman
9. Widen
10. Wyandotte
11. Weimaraner
12. (Jane) Wyatt
13. Wyvern
14. (Andrew) Wyeth

80. IN ALPHABETICAL ORDER
Bucharest

81. INITIAL RESPONSE
Possible answers are shown below. Your answers may differ.
1. Bobolink, buzzard, bluejay, bullfinch; ibis; robin, raven; dove, duck, dodo
2. Foxglove, forget-me-not, fuschia; lily, lady's slipper, lilac, lotus, larkspur; ox-eye daisy, orchid; wisteria, white rose, water lily, witch hazel, windflower; edelweiss, evening primrose; rose, rhododendron
3. Canada, Chile, Cuba, China, Costa Rica, Czech Republic; Oman; Uganda, Uruguay, United States; Niger, Nigeria, Nepal, Norway, Netherlands; Tunisia, Thailand, Turkey; Romania, Rwanda, Russia; Yemen, Yugoslavia

82. WEAREVER
Shoestring

83. SPOONERISMS
1. Climb down, dime clown
2. Sword fight, Ford site
3. Legal rights, regal lights
4. Bright red, right bread
5. Letter box, better locks
6. Rain check, chain wreck
7. Pie tin, tie pin
8. Forty winks, warty finks

84. MIXED NATIONALITIES
Belgian and Bengali

85. A LITTLE R AND R
1. Rough Riders
2. Road Runner
3. Rolling Rock
4. Rocky Road
5. *Ranger Rick*
6. *Rabbit, Run* or *Rabbit Redux*
7. *Red River*
8. "Ramblin' Rose"
9. *Romper Room*
10. Reading Railroad
11. Roy Rogers
12. "Robin Redbreast"
13. *Rob Roy*
14. Ratso Rizzo
15. Russian Revolution

86. CHINESE PUZZLE
Disoriented

87. DROPPIN' G'S
1. Raisin', raisin
2. Muffin', muffin
3. Robbin', Robin
4. Puffin', puffin
5. Vergin', virgin
6. Basin', basin
7. Bobbin', bobbin
8. Brewin', Bruin
9. Gobblin', goblin

88. TO SLEEP, TO SLEEP
Crib-bed

89. A TO Z
1. Zenith
2. Zany
3. Zone
4. Zero or zilch or zip
5. Zigzagging
6. Zombie
7. Zodiacal
8. Zoological
9. Zonked or zzzz
10. Zeppelin

90. J-Q-Z WORD SQUARE
The following are possible answers. Your answer may differ.

```
M A G I     J A M B     N A Z I
A J A R     A Q U A     A X E R
G A Z A     M U S E     Z E T A
I R A Q     B A E Z     I R A Q
```

91. TWO-WAY
1. Draw/ward
2. Gnat/tang or girt/trig
3. Evil/live
4. Golf/flog
5. Plug/gulp
6. Bard/drab
7. Diva/avid
8. Wolf/flow
9. Ogre/ergo
10. Dial/laid, dual/laud
11. Teem/meet, tram/mart
12. Edit/tide, emit/time

92. A LITTLE OFF THE SIDES
Flu (influenza) or tec (detective)

93. MULTINATIONAL TANGLE
1. Iran
2. Peru
3. Oman
4. Mali
5. Spain
6. Nepal
7. Libya
8. Italy
9. Chile
10. China
11. Niger
12. Sudan
13. Yemen
14. Israel
15. Cyprus
16. Angola
17. Algeria
18. Suriname

94. THE SILENT TREATMENT
Raspberry.
Other words with interior silent P's are cupboard and clapboard.

95. OW!
1. Powwow
2. Brownout
3. Countdown
4. Outshout
5. Bauhaus
6. Chow chow
7. Bowwow
8. *Our Town*
9. Loudmouth
10. Found out
11. Southbound
12. Ground round
13. Mau Maus
14. Kowtow or bow down
15. Plow out
16. "How now brown cow"

96. NAME DROPPING
Mongoose to moose

97. THE LONG AND THE SHORT OF IT
1. Leg, league
2. Guess, geese
3. Yelled, yield
4. Beckon, beacon
5. Pressed, priest
6. Berry, beery
7. Sweater, sweeter
8. Chef, sheaf
9. Says, seize
10. Leper, leaper
11. Shelled, shield
12. Pepper, peeper
13. Herring, hearing
14. Many, meanie

98. LOW SCORE WINS
Cabbagehead

99. HINKY-PINKY
1. Go slow
2. Fly high
3. Greek peak
4. Fine wine
5. Great weight
6. Bright light
7. Court sport
8. Deep sleep
9. Breast test
10. Ocean motion

100. INSIDE TRACK
Routine (out, in)

101. WOULD YOU REPEAT THAT?
1. So far, so good
2. One man, one vote or
   One person, one vote
3. Easy come, easy go
4. No pain, no gain
5. Like father, like son
6. New Brunswick, New Jersey
7. "On Dasher! On Dancer!"
8. Another day, another dollar
9. Catch as catch can
10. Star light, star bright
11. *Never Say Never Again*
12. First come, first served
13. Monkey see, monkey do
14. "Come one, come all!"

102. GAG!
Choke and joke

103. THE COMMON TOUCH
1. Pins
2. Bills
3. Jacks or lines
4. Meters
5. Shifts
6. Wings
7. Irons
8. Matches
9. Lines
10. Queens

104. ON THE CONTRARY
Son and daughter

105. UP A TREE
1. Poplar (popular)
2. Willow (will owe)
3. Maple (may pull)
4. Buckeye (buck I)
5. Chestnut (chess nut)
6. Sycamore (sick, a more)
7. Hemlock (him lock)
8. Balsam (bawl some)
9. Aspen (asp in)
10. Cherry (chair he)
11. Witch hazel (which haze'll)
12. Eucalyptus (you clipped us)

106. DOWNSIZING
Queue (Q)

107. FOR FATHER'S DAY

1. Thailand
2. Tiber
3. Tigris
4. Tiebreaker
5. (John) Tyler
6. Tycoon
7. Tylenol
8. Tae kwon do
9. Titus
10. *Typee*
11. Tiger
12. Typhoon
13. Ty-D-bol
14. Ticonderoga
15. Typist
16. (Mike) Tyson
17. Title
18. Tyrant
19. Taiwan
20. Taipei

108. MIDDLEWEIGHT

Shaquille O'Neal

109. CHANGE OF COLOR

1. Blue
2. Gold
3. Pink
4. Gray
5. Ruby
6. Amber or umber
7. Brown
8. Coral
9. Green
10. Ocher
11. Olive
12. Rouge
13. Bronze
14. Cherry
15. Orange
16. Sienna
17. Yellow
18. Scarlet

110. CHANGE OF SHOE

Loafer and furlough

111. B AND B

1. Bib
2. Billy club
3. Blurb
4. Barb
5. Backstab
6. Bulb
7. Beelzebub
8. Bread crumb
9. Bathtub
10. Boob
11. Baobab
12. Bedaub
13. Beachcomb
14. Bear cub
15. Bar tab

112. GOING BACK ON ONE'S WORD

Sponged

113. PAST-TIME

1. Loaded
2. Canned
3. Darned
4. Checked
5. Worsted
6. Belted
7. Flushed
8. Pitched

114. CAPITAL TIME

a) Juneau (June)
b) Augusta (August)

115. N.G.
1. Ping-pong
2. Singsong
3. Sing Sing
4. Wingding
5. Pyongyang
6. Gangling
7. Ding-dong
8. Wang Chung
9. "Bang Bang"
10. Wang Lung
11. Hong Kong
12. Young thing
13. Ringling
14. *King Kong*
15. Ling-Ling and Hsing-Hsing

116. EXTRA SOFT
Ginger

117. TWO FOR TWO
1. Baggage
2. Cadmium
3. Contest
4. Torrent
5. Fanatic
6. Minimum
7. Spangle
8. Elusive
9. Grasped
10. Quivery

118. REPEATING NUMBER
Eighty-eight to nighty-night

119. "A" PUZZLE
1. Await a weight
2. A broad abroad
3. About a bout
4. Around a round
5. A rose arose
6. Attacks a tax
7. Ahead a head
8. A better abettor
9. A noise annoys
10. Accrue a crew
11. A sister's assisters
12. Acquire a quire
13. A rival's arrivals
14. A parent apparent

120. MYSTERY BOOK
It was one volume of an encyclopedia.

121. BLANK OF THE BLANK
1. Lily of the valley
2. *The Last of the Mohicans*
3. Letter of the law
4. Life of the party
5. *The Lord of the Rings*
6. *The Lady of the Lake*
7. Lay of the land
8. Land of the free
9. Law of the jungle
10. Luck of the draw
11. *Lord of the Flies*
12. Lake of the Woods
13. Letters of the alphabet
14. "Leader of the Pack"

122. ON THE UP AND UP
Half-baked

123. SOUNDING PRESIDENTIAL
1. Reagan (ray gun)
2. Taylor (tail her)
3. Arthur (Are there)
4. Lincoln (linkin')
5. Fillmore (fill more)
6. Nixon (Knicks on)
7. Carter (caught her)
8. Eisenhower (eyes and our)

124. IT MIGHT AS WELL BE GREEK
Sci-fi

125. FOOD FOR THOUGHT

The following are our answers. Your answers don't have to match.

1. Don't put all your eggs in one basket.
2. Don't cry over spilt milk.
3. One man's meat is another man's poison.
4. An apple a day keeps the doctor away. The apple doesn't fall far from the tree. One bad apple spoils the barrel.
5. Honey catches more flies than vinegar.
6. Too many cooks spoil the broth.
7. You can't make an omelet without breaking eggs.
8. What's sauce for the goose is sauce for the gander.
9. Guests and fish begin to smell after three days.
10. That's the way the cookie crumbles.
11. You can't have your cake and eat it, too.
12. The proof of the pudding is in the eating.

126. YOU SAID A MOUTHFUL
Twelfth

127. 2-D

1. Dear Diary
2. Done deal
3. *Dirty Dozen*
4. Direct dial or dial direct
5. Disk drive
6. Dog days
7. Double dribble
8. Dirt Devil
9. "Delta Dawn"
10. Donald Duck
11. Dick Deadeye
12. Dr. Dolittle
13. Draft dodger
14. Dry dock
15. Dynamic Duo
16. *Dirty Dancing*
17. Dapper Dan
18. Daily Double

128. COLLEGE MEN
Commencement

129. BROOKLYNESE

1. Hurl, Hoyle
2. Burr, boy
3. Verse, voice
4. Purrs, poise
5. Learn, loin
6. Hearst, hoist
7. Furl, foil
8. First, foist
9. Early, oily
10. Averred, avoid

130. BROOKLYNESE 2
Curl and coil

131. X MARKS THE SPOT

1. Marx, marks
2. Tax, tacks
3. Coax, Cokes
4. Flex, flecks
5. Box, Bach's
6. Nix, Knicks
7. Lax, lacks
8. Rex, wrecks
9. Phlox, flocks
10. Knox, knocks
11. Sax, sacks
12. Bronx, broncs

132. GOING BUGGY
Ant and gnat

133. MIND YOUR P'S AND Q'S

1. Plaque
2. *Pequod*
3. Parquet
4. Piquant
5. Prequel
6. Pop quiz
7. Physique
8. Paraquat
9. Pipsqueak
10. Perquisite
11. Propinquity
12. Picturesque

134. NUMBER, PLEASE
Intended answers: Before, benign, and behalf.
Questionable but clever answers: Betray (be + trey) and beset (be + *sept* [French for seven]).

135. END TO END
1. Tonto
2. Volvo
3. Magma
4. Estes
5. Miami
6. Onion
7. Kafka
8. Aroar
9. Edged
10. Verve
11. At bat
12. Uh-huh
13. "Layla"
14. Casca
15. Salsa

136. SPANISH INQUISITION
Marijuana (Juan and Maria)

137. THE NAME OF THE GAME
1. Bridge
2. Jacks
3. Rummy
4. Tag
5. Twenty questions
6. Checkers
7. Scrabble
8. Poker
9. Ghost
10. Go

138. MEMPHIS
Euphemism

139. TO DO
1. Cuckoo
2. Voodoo
3. Zulu
4. (Desmond) Tutu
5. Yoo-Hoo
6. Choo-choo
7. True-blue
8. Booboo
9. Muumuu
10. Lulu
11. Goo-goo
12. U Nu
13. Pupu
14. Pooh-pooh
15. U2
16. Sulu

140. MUSIC THEORY
Big Band and big bang

141. TWO BY TWO
1. Swallower
2. Shock
3. Maker
4. Horse
5. Robin
6. Flood
7. Mallow
8. Seas
9. Shooter
10. Talk
11. Ink
12. Tuck
13. Shrift or sheet
14. Wheat
15. Still
16. Car or cast
17. Marker
18. Cane
19. Track
20. Sport

142. GUYS
Peter and Paul

143. O BOY!

1. Tam o'shanter
2. Will-o'-the-wisp
3. Twelve o'clock
4. Land O'Lakes
5. Mrs. O'Leary's cow
6. O'Hare
7. Cat-o'-nine-tails
8. Man o' War
9. Leg o' mutton
10. "A Big Hunk O' Love"
11. Peg o' my heart
12. Chock Full O' Nuts or 8 O'Clock
13. Hop-o'-my-thumb
14. Top o' the morning

144. O, NO!

Opossum

145. END ALIKE

1. Birch, larch
2. Glare, stare
3. Fleck, speck
4. After, later
5. Quake, shake
6. Coach, teach
7. Smack, whack
8. Rumba, samba

146. NOVEL WORD LADDER

Two possible answers: Smite, suite, quite, quire, quirk, quark; and smite, spite, spire, spore, sport, aport.

147. FOR YOUR I'S ONLY

1. Grimm, grime
2. Britain, brighten
3. Bicker, biker
4. Still, style
5. Hippo, hypo
6. Hissed, heist
7. Cowlick, cowlike
8. Dipper, diaper
9. Fibber, fiber
10. Sickle, cycle

148. BODY PARTS

Foot (feet) and tooth (teeth)

149. RHYMING TRIOS

1. Snap, crackle, and pop
2. Hook, line, and sinker
3. Red, white, and blue
4. Sun, moon, and stars
5. Ready, willing, and able
6. Game, set, and match
7. Beg, borrow, and steal
8. Runs, hits, and errors
9. Hop, skip, and jump
10. Tom, Dick, and Harry
11. Lock, stock, and barrel
12. Tall, dark, and handsome
13. Blood, sweat, and tears
14. *Bell, Book, and Candle*
15. Ready, aim, and fire
16. Faith, Hope, and Charity
17. Win, place, and show
18. Who, what, and where

150. AUTHOR! AUTHOR!

(Edgar Allan) Poe and (Alexander) Pope

151. A DAY AT THE BEACH

1. Tanager
2. Orangutan
3. Tangier(s)
4. *Titanic*
5. Tandem
6. Rattan
7. Montana
8. "O Tannenbaum!"
9. Caftan
10. Tangram
11. Tantalize
12. Sultana
13. *Tannhauser*
14. Fan-tan
15. Tanzania
16. Satanic

152. TWO-TONE
Instantaneous

153. BRAVING THE ELEMENTS
1. Silver
2. Sulfur
3. Argon
4. Barium
5. Carbon
6. Nickel
7. Cobalt
8. Cesium
9. Arsenic
10. Bromine
11. Bismuth
12. Platinum
13. Nitrogen
14. Strontium

154. PSEUDO-OPPOSITES
Comet and got (come and go)

155. DIS-INFORMATION
1. Disdain (This Dane; "'look with scorn on'")
2. Discord (this chord; "cacophonous combination of notes")
3. Dismayed (This maid; "filled with alarm")
4. Dissuade (this suede; "convince by argument not")
5. Disbarred (This bard; "thrown out")
6. Dismissal (this missile; "firing")
7. Disperse (this purse; "scatter about")
8. Disputer (This pewter; "one who argues a lot")
9. Dissent (This scent; "do not agree")

156. OVERLAPPING STATES
Malaria (Massachusetts, Alabama, Louisiana, Arkansas, Rhode Island, and Iowa)

157. HOW IN-TERESTING
1. Painter
2. Imagine
3. Minutes
4. Villain
5. Swinish
6. Inspire
7. Bassinet
8. Minister
9. Clarinet
10. Bulletin
11. Milliner
12. Faintness
13. Continent
14. Brainless
15. Financier

158. BASEBALL GEAR
Shortstop (shorts + top)

159. WE GET LETTERS
1. A-frame
2. d-Con
3. G-string
4. K-rations
5. V-neck
6. X-ray
7. Q-tips
8. F-stop
9. B-side
10. I-beam
11. Y-axis
12. H-bomb
13. U-Haul
14. E-mail
15. O-ring
16. C-note

160. SCRIPT TEASE
The most common answers: Juxtaposing and jack-in-the-box. A less common answer: ex-journalist. (Note: Juxtaposition has two t's and extrajudicial has two i's.)

161. SHIFTY
1. Scare, scarf
2. Model, modem
3. Convex, convey
4. Muslim, muslin
5. Parsec, parsed
6. Primo, primp
7. Hoover, hooves
8. Marin, Mario
9. Squeak, squeal
10. Hideous, hideout

162. SALTY LANGUAGE
Barnacle, manacle, pinnacle, and tabernacle

163. ONE OR THE OTHER
1. White
2. Yes
3. Fail
4. Tall
5. Sane
6. Fall
7. Rare
8. Bent
9. Stale
10. Tame
11. Play
12. Gay

164. CRYPTO-GEOGRAPHY
Manhattan

165. BE VERY QUIET!
1. Sheepish
2. Hashish
3. Mishmash
4. Shoshone
5. Shipshape
6. Sharpshooter
7. Shellfish
8. Oshkosh
9. Shish-kebab
10. Shoeshine
11. Wishy-washy
12. Shropshire
13. Shrewish
14. Hush-hush

166. A CHANGE OF CLOTHES
Skirt to shirt to shift

167. FORE AND AFT
1. Outshout
2. Underground
3. Restores
4. Ionization
5. Hotshot
6. Entertainment
7. Antiperspirant
8. Xeroxer
9. Bleachable
10. Tormentor
11. Rediscovered
12. *Mesdames*

168. FORE AND AFT 2
(Albert) Einstein

169. CATEGORIES FOR SUMMER
Possible answers are shown below. Your answers may differ.

Items of Furniture B—bed, bench, bookcase, bureau; E—étagère, end table, easy chair; A—armchair, armoire; C—chair, couch, cabinet, chaise, coffee table, credenza, chest of drawers; H—highboy, hassock, highchair, Hoosier cabinet

U.S. Presidents B—Buchanan, Bush; E—Eisenhower; A—Adams, Arthur; C—Coolidge, Clinton, Carter, Cleveland; H—Hayes, Harrison, Harding, Hoover

Basketball Terms B—basket, block, bank shot, baseline, back court, backboard, bench, bucket; E—elbowing, end line; A—air ball, assist, alley oop; C—center, charge, court; H—hoop, hook shot, hand check, half-court line, holding

Current Makes of Cars B—Buick, BMW; E—Eagle; A—Acura, Audi; C—Chevrolet, Chrysler, Cadillac; H—Honda, Hyundai

Cable Channels B—Bravo, Black Entertainment Television; E—ESPN, E!; A—A & E, American Movie Classics; C—CNN, Cinemax, Comedy Channel, CNBC, C-Span; H—HBO, Headline News, Home Shopping Network, History Channel

170. FOUR-LETTER WORDS
All's Well That Ends Well by William Shakespeare

171. SPORTS TALK

1. Strike
2. Birdie
3. Tackle
4. Chip
5. Stroke
6. Check
7. Chop
8. Press
9. Deck
10. Scratch
11. Grand slam
12. Pin

172. A HARD ONE

Wolf + ram

173. SAME OLD SAME OLD

1. Polish
2. Sake
3. Lead
4. Unionized
5. Tarry
6. Wound
7. Minute
8. Entrance

174. JUST DO IT

Dope, dolt, and dodo

175. Q-Z QUIZ

1. Quartz
2. Crazy quilt
3. Queen Elizabeth
4. Squeeze
5. Tranquilize
6. Bezique
7. Quiet Zone
8. Jazz quartet
9. "Suzie Q"
10. *Quatorze*
11. Quezon City
12. *Equalizer*
13. Quetzalcoatl
14. Tariq Aziz
15. Mozambique
16. Queen-size

176. ON VACATION

Labor Day

177. CHEAT SHEET

1. Chin, shin
2. Cheek, chic
3. Cheap, sheep
4. Cherry, sherry
5. Cheddar, shedder
6. Chukker, shucker
7. Charred, shard
8. Chill, shill
9. Chief, sheaf
10. Chair, share
11. Chatter, shatter
12. Chipper, shipper

178. FOUR-"N"-ER

Nonunion

179. INDIAN CORN

1. Mohawk (Moe hawk)
2. Hopi (hope he)
3. Pawnee (pawn he)
4. Delaware (Della wear)
5. Apache (a patchy)
6. Cheyenne (shy Anne)
7. Osage (Oh, sage)
8. Cherokee (chair a key)

180. FOREIGN FOOD

Stuttgart to sugar

181. THREEBIES

1. Baseball bat
2. Baby boom
3. Bible Belt
4. Blow-by-blow
5. Bill Bixby
6. Bubble bath
7. Bob's Big Boy
8. Bobby Brown
9. Boo Boo Bear
10. Bedbugs bite
11. Baby blues
12. Bit by bit
13. Bramble bush
14. "Bye Bye Blackbird"

182. LETTER BANK
Restaurateur

183. INTERNAL BODY PARTS
1. Heart or beard
2. Elegy
3. Aching
4. Tribe
5. Karma or barmy
6. Eclipse or ellipse
7. Delivery
8. Legume
9. Wheelie
10. Anapest
11. Bashing, cashing, dashing, etc.
12. Thankless
13. Orchestra
14. Nanosecond

184. PRESIDENTIAL COUSINS
(Abraham) Lincoln and (Bill) Clinton

185. FALSE RHYMES
1. Wants pants
2. Rear bear
3. Damp swamp
4. Great threat
5. Round wound
6. Tough bough or rough bough
7. Water rater
8. Novel shovel
9. Grown clown
10. Niger tiger
11. Roman woman
12. Most frost
13. Cool wool
14. Plaid maid
15. Whose nose

186. MAKE MINE A DOUBLE
Mug shot.
Other suggested answers: Flute case
(a flute being a tall, slender wineglass),
highball pitcher, and cancan.

187. SEX-CHANGE OPERATIONS
1. Fumble, mumble
2. Fiddle, middle
3. Foment, moment
4. Fixture, mixture
5. Fission, mission
6. Fortified, mortified
7. Forehead, Morehead
8. Forbid, morbid
9. Fountain, mountain
10. Finis, minis

188. MALE AND FEMALE
Bordeaux (boar and doe)

189. A CERTAIN MYSTIQUE
1. Baroque
2. Burlesque
3. Discotheque
4. Clique
5. Plaque
6. Braque
7. Antique
8. Mosque
9. Opaque
10. Grotesque
11. Oblique
12. Basque
13. Mozambique
14. Bezique
15. Dubuque
16. Martinique
17. Boutique
18. Torque
19. Bisque
20. Risqué

190. DIVIDE TO UNITE
Wed and weld

191. AFTER-WORDS
1. Cushion
2. Machine
3. Measure
4. Complex
5. Breaker
6. Station
7. Reading
8. Pudding
9. General
10. Cracker
11. Control
12. Brother

192. HIDDEN OPPOSITES
a) Irk, please
b) Loose, tight

193. SOLVING WITH E'S
1. Streep, strep
2. Reefer, refer
3. Donee, done
4. Career, carer
5. Reenter, renter
6. Meeting, meting
7. Bee sting, besting
8. Commandeer, commander

194. SPORTING CHANCE
Tennis (net)

195. TEEN PROBLEM
1. (Bruce) Springsteen
2. Quarantine
3. Dentyne
4. Nicotine
5. Canteen
6. Sistine
7. Protein
8. Argentine
9. Pristine
10. Guillotine
11. Routine
12. Bactine
13. Saltine
14. Ovaltine
15. Holstein
16. Carotene
17. Florentine
18. Augustine

196. MAKINGS OF A WRITER
J.D. Salinger

197. FINE FUN
1. Fanfare
2. Forfeit
3. Fast-food
4. Fulfill
5. Free-fall
6. Fistfight
7. Far-flung
8. Flatfoot
9. Flimflam
10. Flip-flop
11. Fourfold
12. Freeze-frame
13. Forefront
14. Footfault
15. Force-feed
16. Far-fetched

198. APOSTROPHIZING
Ne'er-do-well.
Other accepted answers: No-man's-land, shoot-'em-ups.

199. END GAME
1. Sparse, spares
2. Mantle, mantel
3. Minuet, minute
4. Louver, Louvre
5. Castor, Castro
6. Cubist, cubits
7. Domain, *domani*
8. Resign, resing
9. Hearts, Hearst
10. Marian, marina
11. Shriek, shrike
12. Mouses, mousse

200. TH-TH-TH-THAT'S ALL, FOLKS!
Asthma or isthmi

WHERE TO HEAR "WEEKEND EDITION SUNDAY"

Nearly 400 NPR stations throughout the U.S. carry *Weekend Edition Sunday*, as this book goes to press. The following guide will help you find the station nearest you. Check your local radio listings (or listen) for program time—Sunday morning in most locales. The puzzle airs at 40 minutes past the hour. Note: All stations are FM except those marked by an asterisk(*).

Alabama
Birmingham—WBHM (90.3)
Dothan—WRWA (88.7)
Gadsen—WSGN (91.5)
Huntsville—WLRH (89.3)
Jacksonville—WLJS (91.9)
Muscle Shoals—WQPR (88.7)
Troy—WTSU (89.9)
Tuscaloosa—WUAL (91.5)

Alaska
Anchorage—KSKA (91.1)
Fairbanks—KUAC (104.7)
Haines—KHNS (102.3)
Homer—KBBI (*890)
Kenai—KDLL (91.9)
Ketchikan—KRBD (105.9)
Kodiak—KMXT (100.1)
Petersburg—KFSK (100.9)
Sitka—KCAW (104.7)
Talkeetna—KTNA (88.5)
Valdez—KCHU (*770)

Arizona
Flagstaff—KNAU (88.7)
Phoenix—KJZZ (91.5)
Tuba City—KGHR (91.5)
Tucson—KUAT (*1550)
Tucson—KUAZ (89.1)
Yuma—KAWC (*1320)
Yuma—KAWC (88.9)

Arkansas
El Dorado—KBSA (90.9)
Fayetteville—KUAF (91.3)
Little Rock—KUAR (89.1)

California
Arcata—KHSU (90.5)
Bakersfield—KPRX (89.1)
Burney—KNCA (89.7)
Chico—KCHO (91.7)
El Centro—KUBO (88.7)
Fresno—KVPR (89.3)
Indio—KCRY (89.3)
Mt. Shasta—KNSQ (88.1)
Oxnard—KCRU (89.1)
Pasadena—KPCC (89.3)

Philo—KZYX (90.7)
Redding—KFPR (88.9)
Rohnert Park—KRCB (91.1)
Sacramento—KXJZ (88.9)
San Bernardino—KVCR (91.9)
San Diego—KPBS (89.5)
San Francisco—KQED (88.5)
San Luis Obispo—KCBX (90.1)
Santa Cruz—KUSP (88.9)
Santa Monica—KCRW (89.9)
Stockton—KUOP (91.3)
Thousand Oaks—KCLU (88.3)
Yreka—KNYR (91.3)

Colorado
Alamosa—KRZA (88.7)
Aspen—KAJX (91.5)
Colorado Springs—KRCC (91.5)
Crested Butte—KBUT (90.3)
Denver—KCFR (90.1)
Grand Junction—KPRN (89.5)
Greeley—KUNC (91.5)
Ignacio—KSUT (91.3)
Paonia—KVNF (90.9)
Telluride—KOTO (91.7)
Vail—KPRE (89.9)

Florida
Fort Myers—WSFP (90.1)
Fort Pierce—WQCS (88.9)
Gainesville—WUFT (89.1)
Melbourne—WFIT (89.5)
Miami—WLRN (91.3)
Pensacola—WUWF (88.1)
Tallahassee—WFSU (88.9)
Tampa—WUSF (89.7)
West Palm Beach—WXEL (90.7)

Georgia
Albany—WUNV (91.7)
Athens—WUGA (91.7)
Augusta—WACG (90.7)
Brunswick—WWIO (89.1)
Columbus—WTJB (91.7)
Fort Gaines—WJWV (90.9)
Macon—WDCO (89.7)
Savannah—WSVH (91.1)
Tifton—WABR (91.1)

Valdosta—WWET (91.7)
Warm Springs—WJSP (88.1)
Waycross—WXVS (90.1)

Guam
Mangiloa—KPRG (89.3)

Hawaii
Honolulu—KIPO (89.3)
Pearl City—KIFO (*1380)

Idaho
Boise—KBSX (91.5)
Cottonwood—KNWO (90.1)
Moscow—KRFA (91.7)
Rexburg—KRIC (100.5)
Twin Falls—KBSW (91.7)

Illinois
Carbondale—WSIU (91.9)
Chicago—WBEZ (91.5)
Griggsville—WIPA (89.3)
Macomb—WIUM (91.3)
Normal—WGLT (89.1)
Olney—WUSI (90.3)
Quincy—WQUB (90.3)
Rock Island—WVIK (90.3)
Rockford—WNIJ (90.5)
Springfield—WSSU (91.9)
Urbana—WILL (*580)

Indiana
Bloomington—WFIU (103.7)
Elkhart—WVPE (88.1)
Evansville—WNIN (88.3)
Indianapolis—WFYI (90.1)
Muncie—WBST (92.1)
Richmond—WVXR (89.3)

Iowa
Ames—WOI (*640)
Cedar Falls—KUNI (90.9)
Council Bluffs—KIWR (89.7)
Decorah—KLNI (88.7)
Fort Dodge—KTPR (91.1)
Iowa City—WSUI (*910)
Mason City—KUNY (91.5)
Sioux City—KWIT (90.3)

Kansas
Garden City—KANZ (91.1)
Great Bend—KHCT (90.9)
Hill City—KZNA (90.5)
Hutchinson—KHCC (90.1)
Lawrence—KANU (91.5)
Pittsburg—KRPS (89.9)
Salina—KHCD (89.5)

Kentucky
Bowling Green—WKYU (88.9)
Elizabethtown—WKUE (90.9)
Hazard—WEKH (90.9)
Henderson—WKPB (89.5)
Lexington—WUKY (91.3)
Louisville—WFPL (89.3)
Morehead—WMKY (90.3)
Murray—WKMS (91.3)
Richmond—WEKU (88.9)
Somerset—WDCL (89.7)

Louisiana
Alexandria—KLSA (90.7)
Baton Rouge—WRKF (89.3)
Monroe—KEDM (90.3)
New Orleans—WWNO (89.9)
Shreveport—KDAQ (89.9)

Maine
Bangor—WMEH (90.9)
Calais—WMED (89.7)
Fort Kent—WMEF (106.5)
Portland—WMEA (90.1)
Presque Isle—WMEM (106.1)
Waterville—WMEW (91.3)

Maryland
Baltimore—WJHU (88.1)
Salisbury—WSCL (89.5)

Massachusetts
Boston—WBUR (90.9)
Great Barrington—
    WAMQ (105.1)
Harwich—WCCT (90.3)
Sandwich—WSDH (91.5)
West Barnstable—WKKL (90.7)

Michigan
Alpena—WCML (91.7)
Ann Arbor—WUOM (91.7)
Bay City—WUCX (90.1)
Detroit—WDET (101.9)
East Lansing—WKAR (*870)
Flint—WFUM (91.1)
Grand Rapids—WGVU (*1480)
Grand Rapids—WGVU (88.5)

Grand Rapids—WVGR (104.1)
Harbor Springs—WCMW (103.9)
Kalamazoo—WMUK (102.1)
Manistee—WVXM (97.7)
Marquette—WNMU (90.1)
Mt. Pleasant—WCMU (89.5)
Sault Ste. Marie—WCMZ (98.3)
Ypsilanti—WEMU (89.1)

Minnesota
Austin—KMSK (91.3)
Bemidji—KNBJ (91.3)
Collegeville—KNSR (88.9)
Duluth—WSCN (100.5)
Grand Rapids—KAXE (91.7)
La Crescent—KXLC (91.1)
Mankato—KMSU (89.7)
Moorhead—KCCD (90.3)
Rochester—KZSE (90.7)
St. Paul—KNOW (91.1)
St. Peter—KNGA (91.5)
Thief River Falls—KNTN (102.7)

Mississippi
Biloxi—WMAH (90.3)
Booneville—WMAE (89.5)
Bude—WMAU (88.9)
Greenwood—WMAO (90.9)
Jackson—WMPN (91.3)
Meridian—WMAW (88.1)
Mississippi St.—WMAB (89.9)
Oxford—WMAV (90.3)
Senatobia—WKNA (88.9)

Missouri
Cape Girardeau—KRCU (90.9)
Chillicothe—KRNW (88.9)
Columbia—KBIA (91.3)
Kansas City—KCUR (89.3)
Maryville—KXCV (90.5)
Point Look—KSMS (90.5)
Rolla—KUMR (88.5)
Springfield—KSMU (91.1)
St. Louis—KWMU (90.7)
Warrensburg—KCMW (90.9)

Montana
Billings—KEMC (91.7)
Bozeman—KBMC (102.1)
Great Falls—KGPR (89.9)
Havre—KNMC (90.1)
Miles City—KECC (90.7)
Missoula—KUFM (89.1)

North Carolina
Asheville—WCQS—(88.1)
Chapel Hill—WUNC (91.5)

Charlotte—WFAE (90.7)
Fayetteville—WFSS (89.1)
Franklin—WFQS (91.3)
Spindale—WNCW (88.7)

North Dakota
Bismarck—KCND (90.5)
Dickinson—KDPR (89.9)
Fargo—KDSU (91.9)
Grand Forks—KFJM (*1370)
Grand Forks—KFJM (89.3)
Jamestown—KPRJ (93.5)
Minot—KMPR (88.9)
Williston—KPPR (89.5)

Nebraska
Alliance—KTNE (91.1)
Bassett—KMNE (90.3)
Chadron—KCNE (91.9)
Hastings—KHNE (89.1)
Lexington—KLNE (88.7)
Lincoln—KUCV (90.9)
Merriman—KRNE (91.5)
Norfolk—KXNE (89.3)
North Platte—KPNE (91.7)
Omaha—KIOS (91.5)

Nevada
Elko—KNCC (91.5)
Las Vegas—KNPR (89.5)
Panaca—KLNR (91.7)
Reno—KUNR (88.7)
Tonopah—KTPH (91.7)

New Hampshire
Concord—WEVO (89.1)
Hanover—WEVH (91.3)
Keene—WEVN (90.7)

New Mexico
Albuquerque—KUNM (89.9)
Gallup—KGLP (91.7)
Las Cruces—KRWG (90.7)
Maljamar—KMTH (98.7)
Portales—KENW (89.5)
Ramah-Pine Hill—KTDB (89.7)

New York
Albany—WAMC (90.3)
Binghamton—WSKG (89.3)
Blue Mtn. Lake—WXLH (89.9)
Buffalo—WBFO (88.7)
Buffalo—WNED (*970)
Canajoharie—WCAN (93.3)
Canton—WSLU (89.5)
Geneva—WEOS (89.7)
Ithaca—WSQG (90.9)

New York (continued)
Jamestown—WUBJ (88.1)
Jeffersonville—WJFF (90.5)
Kingston—WAMK (90.9)
Malone—WSLO (90.9)
Middletown—WOSR (91.7)
New York—WNYC (*820)
New York—WNYC (93.9)
North Creek—WXLG (89.9)
Olean—WOLN (91.3)
Oneonta—WSQC (91.7)
Oswego—WRVO (89.9)
Peru—WXLU (88.3)
Rochester—WXXI (*1370)
Saranac Lake—WSLL (90.5)
Ticonderoga—WANC (103.9)
Utica—WRVN (91.9)
Watertown—WRVJ (91.7)
Watertown—WSLJ (88.5)

Ohio
Athens—WOUB (*1340)
Athens—WOUB (91.3)
Cambridge—WOUC (89.1)
Chillicothe—WOUH (91.9)
Chillicothe—WVXC (89.3)
Cincinnati—WVXU (91.7)
Cleveland—WCPN (90.3)
Columbus—WCBE (90.5)
Columbus—WOSU (*820)
Dover—WKRJ (91.5)
Ironton—WOUL (89.1)
Kent—WKSU (89.7)
Lima—WGLE (90.7)
Mt. Gilead—WVXG (95.1)
Oxford—WMUB (88.5)
Toledo—WGTE (91.3)
West Union—WVXW (89.5)
Wooster—WKRW (89.3)
Youngstown—WYSU (88.5)
Zanesville—WOUZ (90.1)

Oklahoma
Lawton—KCCU (89.3)
Norman—KGOU (106.3)
Oklahoma City—KROU (105.7)
Stillwater—KOSU (91.7)
Tulsa—KWGS (89.5)

Oregon
Ashland—KSMF (89.1)
Ashland—KSOR (90.1)
Bend—KOAB (91.3)
Coos Bay—KSBA (88.5)
Corvallis—KOAC (*550)
Eugene—KLCC (89.7)
Klamath Falls—KSKF (90.9)
Newport—KLCO (90.5)
Pendleton—KRBM (90.9)
Portland—KOPB (91.5)
Roseburg—KSRS (91.5)

Pennsylvania
Bethlehem—WDIY (88.1)
Erie—WQLN (91.3)
Harrisburg—WITF (89.5)
Kane—WPSB (90.1)
Philadelphia—WHYY (90.9)
Pittsburgh—WDUQ (90.5)
Scranton—WVIA (89.9)
University Park—WPSU (91.9)

South Carolina
Aiken—WLJK (89.1)
Beaufort—WJWJ (89.9)
Columbia—WLTR (91.3)
Conway—WHMC (90.1)
Greenville—WEPR (90.1)
Mt. Pleasant—WSCI (89.3)
Rock Hill—WNSC (88.9)
Sumter—WRJA (88.1)

South Dakota
Brookings—KESD (88.3)
Faith—KPSD (97.1)
Lowry—KQSD (91.9)
Martin—KZSD (102.5)
Pierpont—KDSD (90.9)
Rapid City—KBHE (89.3)
Reliance—KTSD (91.1)
Sioux Falls—KCSD (90.9)
Sioux Falls—KNSW (91.7)
Vermillion—KUSD (89.7)

Tennessee
Collegedale—WSMC (90.5)
Dyersburg—WKNQ (90.7)
Jackson—WKNP (90.1)
Johnson City—WETS (89.5)
Memphis—WKNO (91.1)
Murfreesboro—WMOT (89.5)
Nashville—WPLN (90.3)

Texas
Abilene—KACU (89.7)
Austin—KUT (90.5)
Beaumont—KVLU (91.3)
College Station—KAMU (90.9)
Corpus Christi—KEDT (90.3)
Dallas—KERA (90.1)
El Paso—KTEP (88.5)
Harlingen—KMBH (88.9)
Houston—KUHF (88.7)
Lufkin—KLDN (88.9)
McAllen—KHID (88.1)
Odessa—KOCV (91.3)
San Antonio—KSTX (89.1)
Texarkana—KTXK (91.5)

Utah
Logan—KUSU (91.5)
Park City—KCPW (88.3)
Salt Lake City—KUER (90.1)

Vermont
Burlington—WVPS (107.9)
Rutland—WRVT (88.7)
Windsor—WVPR (89.5)

Virginia
Charlottesville—WVTU (89.3)
Crozet—WMRY (103.5)
Harrisonburg—WMRA (90.7)
Lexington—WMRL (89.9)
Marion—WVTR (91.9)
Norfolk—WHRV (89.5)
Norfolk—WNSB (91.1)
Richmond—WCVE (88.9)
Roanoke—WVTF (89.1)

Washington
Bellingham—KZAZ (91.7)
Ellensburg—KNWR (90.7)
Pullman—KWSU (*1250)
Richland—KFAE (89.1)
Seattle—KUOW (94.9)
Tacoma—KPLU (88.5)
Yakima—KNWY (90.3)

Wisconsin
Brule—WHSA (89.9)
Eau Claire—WUEC (89.7)
Green Bay—WPNE (89.3)
Hayward—WOJB (88.9)
Kenosha—WGTD (91.1)
LaCrosse—WLSU (88.9)
Madison—WERN (88.7)
Menomonie—WVSS (90.7)
Milwaukee—WUWM (89.7)
Wausau—WHRM (90.9)

Wyoming
Jackson—KUWJ (90.3)
Laramie—KUWR (91.9)
Rock Springs—KUWZ (90.5)